Lan

LA GOMERA
and
SOUTHERN TENERIFE

a countryside guide
Seventh edition

Noel Rochford

Seventh edition © 2016
Sunflower Books™
PO Box 36160
London SW7 3WS UK
www.sunflowerbooks.co.uk

Sunflower Books and
'Landscapes' are Registered
Trademarks.

ISBN 978-1-85691-483-3

At Los Aceviños

Important note to the reader

We have tried to ensure that the descriptions and maps in this book are error-free at press date. The book will be updated, where necessary, whenever future printings permit. It will be very helpful for us to receive your comments (sent in care of the publishers, please) for the updating of future printings.

We also rely on those who use this book — especially walkers — to take along a good supply of common sense when they explore. Conditions change fairly rapidly in the Canary Islands, and *storm damage or bulldozing may make a route unsafe at any time*. If the route is not as we outline it here, and your way ahead is not secure, return to the point of departure. *Never attempt to complete a tour or walk under hazardous conditions!* Please read carefully the notes on pages 35-43 and the introductory comments at the beginning of each tour and walk (regarding road conditions, equipment, grade, distances and time, etc). Explore *safely*, while at the same time respecting the beauty of the countryside.

Cover photograph: Chejelipes, in the Barranco de Las Lajas (Car tour 5)
Title page: Roque de la Zarcita, with El Teide on Tenerife in the distance

Photographs: the author, except for pages 16, 61 (Andreas Stieglitz); 23, 48 (Pat Underwood), 69, 73, 80, 83, 88 (middle), 89, 104 (bottom), 114, 115 (Conny Spelbrink); 76-7, 68 and cover (Shutterstock)
Drawings: Sharon Rochford
Maps: Sunflower Books, originally based on maps of the Servicio Geográfico del Ejército
A CIP catalogue record for this book is available from the British Library.
Printed and bound in England: Short Run Press, Exeter

Contents

Preface   5
   Acknowledgements; Useful books   6

Getting about   7

Picnicking   8
   Picnic suggestions   9

Touring   12

   **TOUR 1: LAS CAÑADAS AND THE NORTHWEST
   (TENERIFE)**   13
     Playa de las Américas • Vilaflor • Las Cañadas •
     La Orotava • Puerto de la Cruz • Icod de los Vinos •
     Buenavista • Punta de Teno • Masca • Santiago del Teide
     • Los Gigantes • San Juan • Playa de las Américas

   **TOUR 2: THE CUMBRE AND THE SUN-BAKED
   SOUTH (TENERIFE)**   18
     Playa de las Américas • Guía de Isora • Las Cañadas •
     El Portillo • Güimar • Arico • Granadilla
     • Playa de las Américas

   **TOUR 3: QUIET CORNERS OF THE NORTHEAST
   (TENERIFE)**   20
     Playa de las Américas • Tacoronte • Bajamar •
     Punta del Hidalgo • Cruz del Carmen • Las Carboneras •
     Taborno • Pico del Inglés •La Laguna • Playa de
     las Américas

   **TOUR 4: BUCOLIC CHARMS OF THE
   RUGGED ANAGA (TENERIFE)**   22
     Playa de las Américas • Pico del Inglés • Roque Negro •
     El Bailadero • Chamorga • Taganana • Almáciga •
     Benijo • San Andrés • Igueste • Santa Cruz •
     Playa de las Américas

   TOUR 5: LA GOMERA'S SOUTHERN LANDSCAPES   24
     Valle Gran Rey • Arure • Las Hayas • Chipude •
     Alajeró • Playa de Santiago • San Sebastián • El Cedro
     • Los Roques • Laguna Grande • Valle Gran Rey

   TOUR 6: LA GOMERA'S VERDANT NORTH   30
     Valle Gran Rey • Las Hayas • Laguna Grande •
     Hermigua • Agulo • Garajonay National Park Visitors'
     Centre • Vallehermoso • Arure • Valle Gran Rey

Walking   35
   Guides, signposting and waymarking, maps   36
   Dogs — and other nuisances   37
   Weather   37
   Where to stay   38
   What to take   39
   Country code for walkers and motorists   40

Spanish for walkers   41
Walkers' checklist   42
Organisation of the walks   43

WALKS ON TENERIFE (🚌) walks suitable for
motorists; see page 35)

🚌 1 Montaña Guaza   44
🚌 2 Roque del Conde   47
🚌 3 Adeje • Barranco del Infierno • Adeje   50
🚌 4 Adeje • Boca del Paso • Ifonche • La Escalona   53
🚌 5 Boca Tauce • Montaña del Cedro • Boca Tauce   56
🚌 6 Parador de las Cañadas • Paisaje Lunar • Vilaflor   59
🚌 7 Araza • La Cabezada • Araza   64
🚌 8 Masca • Barranco de Masca • Playa de Masca • Masca   66

WALKS ON LA GOMERA (🚌) walks suitable for
motorists; see page 35)

🚌 9 Barranco de Arure   69
🚌 10 From Valle Gran Rey to Arure   72
🚌 11 Arure • Ermita San Salvador • Arure   74
🚌 12 Arure • Las Hayas • Los Granados   77
🚌 13 Chipude • Ermita Nuestra Señora de Guadalupe •
       Valle Gran Rey   81
🚌 14 Lomo del Balo • La Vizcaína • Chipude • La Fortaleza •
       Chipude   84
🚌 15 Cruce de la Zarcita • El Cedro • Garajonay • Chipude   86
   16 El Rumbazo • (Targa) • Playa de Santiago   89
   17 Pajarito • Imada • Guarimiar • El Rumbazo   91
🚌 18 Pastrana • Benchijigua • Imada • Alajeró road   94
🚌 19 Degollada de Peraza • La Laja • Roque de Agando •
       Degollada de Peraza   99
🚌 20 Degollada de Peraza • Seima • Casas de Contrera •
       Degollada de Peraza   101
   21 San Sebastián • Playa de la Guancha • El Cabrito •
       Playa de Santiago   103
🚌 22 Camino Forestal de Majona to San Sebastián   106
🚌 23 Hermigua • Enchereda • Las Casetas (Mirador
       A Lazcano)   110
🚌 24 Hermigua • El Cedro • Hermigua   115
🚌 25 Agulo • Centro de Visitantes Juego de Bolas • Embalse
       de Amalahuigue • El Tión • Vallehermoso   118
🚌 26 Vallehermoso • La Meseta • Chorros de Epina •
       Vallehermoso   123
🚌 27 Vallehermoso • Ermita Santa Clara • Playa de
       Vallehermoso • Vallehermoso   125

Appendix   129
   Tourist information   129
   Bus, plane and ferry timetables   129

Index   134

Island maps and town plans   *inside back cover*
   with plans of Los Cristianos/Playa de las Américas
   (Tenerife) and San Sebastián (La Gomera)

Drawings of island flora   42, 51

● Preface

Few places in the world can offer the kaleidoscope of natural beauty found in the Canary Islands. What one island lacks, another has in plenty. Each island has a personality of its own — as you will see if you use this book to explore *both* La Gomera and Tenerife.

Over the years, people have asked me why this book is not devoted *solely* to La Gomera (admittedly, my favourite Canary Island). The reason is simple: since there are no direct flights from the UK or northern Europe to the island, most people fly to Reina Sofia airport in the south of Tenerife and go on to Gomera by ferry from the nearby port at Los Cristianos. So if you are going via Tenerife anyway, why not spend some time there and see the best of it? That's the way this book is presented — starting with tours and walks on Tenerife, the guide moves on to explore La Gomera.

The south of Tenerife is associated with bodies and beaches. Few visitors explore beyond the 'compulsory' coach tour to El Teide. They may return home thinking of Tenerife's landscape as barren, however magnificent. They have missed the laurel forests of the Anaga and the soft green valleys of the Teno Peninsula. The car tours described in this book put the *entire island* within easy reach. *Do* get out and explore — you'll be surprised! You may even be enticed to return and get to know the whole island in depth. If so, my companion guide, *Landscapes of Tenerife* (also published by Sunflower) will put picnic strolls and walks in the Teno and Anaga peninsulas, La Orotava and Las Cañadas at your fingertips.

Few people think of walking in the south of Tenerife, because the bleached façade of the interior looks rather unappealing from the coast, and in summer it can be very hot and sunny. But during the winter months some days will be cool and cloudy, and they're ideal for walking. The eight walks in the south of the island described here lead to exhilarating beauty spots — two of Tenerife's top walks, but the other six less well known. You'll venture upon canyon-sized ravines, gorges overflowing with vegetation, waterfalls and trickling streams — all well concealed in this supposedly 'bleak' landscape. These walks have been chosen for their easy access from the south.

5

When you've explored a bit on Tenerife, move on to La Gomera. Tantalizingly close, this little dome-shaped island sits some 20 miles southwest of Los Cristianos — just 50 minutes away by high-speed ferry. The ferry schedules allow you enough time to go even for one day's touring or walking — but I recommend *at least* a week.

La Gomera is a total contrast to the *playas* of southern Tenerife. It's a place where people go to appreciate the simple things in life — peace and quiet, space to breathe and splendid rural scenery. In all three of these it excels, and, on top of this, the island remains largely unspoilt.

La Gomera is a walkers' paradise. But if you're not a walker, explore the island by car. Break up your tours with picnics or leg-stretching breaks along the paths to the picnic spots suggested on pages 10 and 11. Many of these picnic settings lie along the route of a long walk, so you can get the 'feel' of the landscape without hiking for miles. Perhaps, unawares, you will find yourself drawn deeper and deeper into the countryside.

Getting to know an island is getting to know the people, so before you set off, learn a few words of Spanish. The 'Gomeros' are a reserved people. However, if you do speak some Spanish, you will find them responsive and helpful. (It's not likely that you'll have time to master the other 'language' spoken on La Gomera — the *silbo*, a centuries-old 'whistling language' developed by the Guanches to communicate across the enormous ravines that slice through the island.)

Whether you are exploring Tenerife, La Gomera, or both islands, this book will help you to *find* something different, *taste* something different, and to *meet* someone different — the essence, I hope, of a memorable visit.

Acknowledgements

My special thanks to my publishers, who revised this Seventh edition just prior to publication, but especially to Conny Spelbrink, who rewalked all the routes for the Sixth edition (2014). Conny, for her part, would like to thank two lovely hotels on Gomera, both of which she heartily recommends: the Parador de la Gomera in San Sebastián (see photograph opposite) and the Hotel Gran Rey in Valle Gran Rey.

Useful books

There are many general guides devoted to Tenerife, but just one or two to La Gomera. Try to buy a copy of *Wild flowers of the Canary Islands* by David and Zoe Bramwell on the web before travelling.

Also available: Landscapes of Tenerife (Teno • Orotava • Anaga • Cañadas), Landscapes of Gran Canaria, Landscapes of Lanzarote, Landscapes of Fuerteventura, Landscapes of La Palma and El Hierro. All by Noel Rochford and published by Sunflower Books.

❀ Getting about

Tenerife

The best way to get around the island is by **hiring a car** (or motorbike). **Coach tours** are also a popular way of seeing Tenerife. While **taxis** cater for those with less time and more money, sharing can make them worthwhile.

If you're not pushed for time, the local **buses run by Titsa (www.titsa.com)** are fun and inexpensive — invest in fare-saving travel cards, valid on the tram and all bus lines except 342 and 348 to Teide. The plan on the touring map inside the back cover shows bus stations and some major stops in the southern tourist centres. The bus network is very extensive, but if you're going far from your base in the south, schedules may not permit you to take *long* walks: you may need to arrange alternative transport.

La Gomera

If you only spend a day or two, a **hire car** is the best way of getting about. If you're visiting from Tenerife, you can either take your car over or hire a car in San Sebastián (near the port or in town). If you're going straight to Gomera, it should be cheaper to arrange car hire at home before you travel. **Taxis** are another option, but agree on the price before setting out or make sure they switch on the meter.

Local **buses (www.guaguagomera.com)** run in conjunction with ferry arrivals/departures. Morning buses come from all around the island to bring passengers for the first ferry departure, return to the villages with arrivals from Tenerife, travel back to the port, etc. This limited service is adequate for most of the walks and picnics.

Gomera's Parador sits just at the edge of the cliffs in San Sebastián, with views across to Teide on Tenerife.

❀ Picnicking ─────────

Picnickers are extremely well catered for on both Tenerife and La Gomera. The authorities have set up several well-equipped 'recreation areas' around the islands. All have been laid out in harmony with their surroundings. At these *zonas recreativas* (which tend to be crowded on weekends and holidays), you'll find tables, benches and drinking fountains. Many are also equipped with barbecues, WCs and play areas for children. All **roadside** picnic areas **with tables** (and sometimes other facilities) are indicated in the touring notes and on the touring maps by the symbol ⊼. The facilities available are listed in the picnic notes.

This book also includes many other suggestions — for picnics 'off the beaten track', along the path of a walk. Five are included for Tenerife and 14 for La Gomera (there are some 37 others in the companion volume, *Landscapes of Tenerife*). All the information you need to get to the suggested picnic spots is given on the following pages, where *picnic numbers correspond to walk numbers:* you can quickly find the general location on the island by referring to the appropriate pull-out touring map (which shows where the walks are located). Most of these picnics are very easy to reach, and I outline transport details (🚐: which bus to take; 🚗: where to park), how long it will take you to walk to the picnic spot, and views or setting. Beneath the picnic title, you will also find a map reference: the location of the picnic spot is shown on this large-scale *walking* map by the symbol *P*, printed in green. Some of the picnic settings are also illustrated.

Please glance over the comments before you start off on your picnic: if some walking is involved, remember to wear sensible shoes and to **take a sunhat** (○ indicates a picnic in *full sun*). It's a good idea to take along a plastic sheet as well, in case the ground is damp or prickly.

If you're travelling to your picnic by bus, be sure to verify bus departure times in advance. Although there are timetables at the back of the book (starting on page 129), they *do* change from time to time, without prior warning. **If you are travelling to your picnic by car**, do park *well off* the road!

All picnickers should read the Country code on page 40 and go quietly in the countryside.

Tenerife

4 IFONCHE (map pages 52-53, photograph page 55)

by car only: 20-30min on foot

🚗 Park near Restaurante El Dornajo in Ifonche, 3.5km west of La Escalona, on the TF51. Detour on Car tour 1

Follow Short walk 4 (page 53) as far as the top of the crest overlooking the impressive Barranco del Infierno. Shade of pines

5 BOCA TAUCE (map page 57, photograph page 58, bottom)

by car: 15-20min on foot
by bus: 15-20min on foot

🚗 Parking area at Boca Tauce. Car tours 1 and 2

🚌 to Boca Tauce

Follow Walk 5 (page 56) to reach the lava flow, an interesting, unfrequented corner of Las Cañadas. Shade of pines

6 PIEDRAS AMARILLAS (map pages 60-61) ○

by car: 15-20min on foot
by bus: 15-20min on foot

🚗 (Car tours 1 and 2) or 🚌 to the Parador de las Cañadas

Follow Walk 6 (page 59), to the 'Yellow Stones' (no shade).

7 ARAZA (map page 65) ○

by car: 5-30min on foot
by bus: 5-30min on foot

🚗 Parking for 2-3 cars at the look-out point just above the track to Araza, a farmstead (this is the *only* gravel track branching off west between Santiago del Teide and Masca). Car tour 1

🚌 to the Araza turn-off

You can picnic at the outlook over the Masca Valley (a minute up the right-hand fork at the outset of the hike) or continue further along the ridge for more breathtaking views. No shade

8 BARRANCO DE MASCA (map pages 66-67, nearby photo pages 12-13)

by car: 25-30min on foot
by bus: 25-30min on foot

🚗 (Car tour 1) or 🚌 to Masca village

Follow Walk 8 (page 66), to picnic just before the bridge. Shade from rocks and nearby palms. Wear stout shoes; the paths are very slippery once you leave the village. Expect company; this is a popular walk!

Tenerife's *zonas recreativas*

(See touring map of Tenerife for 🏕-symbol. All have shade, tables, benches, water; settings described in the appropriate car tours.)

LA CALDERA (Car tour 1)
Barbecues, play area, toilets, bar/restaurant

LAS CAÑADAS ROAD (Car tour 1) Six sites between Aguamansa and El Portillo, all signposted. Only Zona Recreativa Ramón Caminero has barbecues (and camping facilities). One of the sites is just by the famous 'stone daisy' (Margarita de Piedra).

PICO DE LAS FLORES (Car tour 2) Tables and benches; west of La Esperanza

CHANAJIGA (near Car tour 1)
South of Los Realejos; barbecues; pine wood setting with wooden bridges, etc; toilets

EL LAGAR (near Car tour 1)
Just above La Guancha; barbecues, toilets

LAS ARENAS NEGRAS (near Car tour 1) South of Icod de los Vinos; rough track; unusual black sand area; barbecues, toilets

LAS LAJAS (Car tour 1)

CHIO (Car tour 2)

MONTE LOS FRAILES (Car tour 2) In a pine wood

La Gomera

9 BARRANCO DE ARURE (map pages 70-71, photograph page 69)

by car or taxi: up to 20min on foot
by bus: up to 20min on foot
🚗 or 🚌 to Casa de la Seda. Car tours 5 and 6
Follow Walk 9 (page 69) as far as you like into the lush Arure ravine.
Note: this walk is always busy. Shade

10 MIRADOR ERMITA DEL SANTO (map pages 70-71)

by car: up to 5min on foot
by bus: 10-15min on foot
🚗 Mirador Ermita del Santo. Car tours 5 and 6
🚌 to Bar/Restaurant El Jape, just below Arure. Follow the road towards the village, then take the first road off left.
Breathtaking views over the hamlet of Taguluche. Shade of pines

11 ERMITA SAN SALVADOR (map pages 70-71, photograph page 75)

by car only: no walking
🚗 Park at the chapel (Ermita San Salvador) in Taguluche (detour on Car tour 6). Passing through the village, take the first turn-off right (signposted).
Full zona recreativa facilities. Severe but dramatic scenery.

12 LAS HAYAS (map pages 70-71, photograph page 80) ○

by car or taxi: 20-30min on foot
by bus: 20-30min on foot
🚗 Park at La Montaña Restaurant. Car tours 5 and 6

Roque de Agando pierces through the clouds below the Garajonay summit.

🚌 Valle Gran Rey bus to La Montaña restaurant at Las Hayas.
Use the notes on page 80, from the 1h05min-point, to reach the spectacular outlook over the Gran Rey Valley. No immediate shade. Allow plenty of time for the climb back up, if you are catching a bus.

14 LA FORTALEZA (map pages 70-71, photograph page 31) ○

by car or taxi: 10min on foot
by bus: 20-30min on foot
🚗 Park at the foot of the concrete lane forking east off the La Dama road in Pavón, just below La Fortaleza. Car tour 5
🚌 Get off the bus just past the La Dama turn-off.
Use the map to reach the outlook over the Barranco de Erque. No shade

15 GARAJONAY SUMMIT (map pages 96-97, photograph below)

by car: 20-25min on foot
by bus: 25-35min on foot
🚗 Park at Alto del Contadero. Car tours 5 and 6. 🚌 to the Pajarito junction
By car, follow Short walk 15-2 on page 86 from Alto del Contadero. Travelling by bus, alight at the Pajarito junction and follow Alternative walk 17 on page 91 to reach the summit. The viewpoint platform provides limited wind protection, and a few nearby pines offer shade. On cloudless days all of La Gomera and the other Canaries can be seen.

16 TARGA (map pages 96-97) ○

by car: 5-10min on foot
by bus: 15-20min on foot
🚗 Park neatly in Targa. Car tour 5. 🚌 to the Targa turn-off, then on foot.
Follow the road bearing right off the road into the village. Barely three minutes along, climb the signposted trail on the left. A couple of minutes over the pass you reach an 'eagle's perch' with magnificent views. Shade only from the valley walls.

17 CASETA DE LOS NORUEGOS (map pages 96-97)

by car: 15-20min on foot
by bus: 15-20min on foot
🚗 (Car tours 5 and 6) or 🚌 to the turn-off for the 'Caseta de los Noruegos', a wide, heavily sign-posted junction 100m east of the KM22 road marker on the GM2. *Follow Walk 17 from the 20min-point to the 35min-point, for a good view across the Barranco de Benchijigua to Roque de Agando.*

18 PASTRANA (map pages 96-97)

by car only: 15-20min on foot
🚗 Pastrana (Detour on Car tour 5) *Follow Walk 18 (page 95) as far as the gofio mill. A lovely spot, deep in a valley. Limited shade*

19 MIRADOR DEGOLLADA DE PERAZA (map pages 96-97) ○

by car: up to 10min on foot
by bus: up to 10min on foot
🚗 Park at Bar Peraza, near the *mirador* on the GM2. Car tour 5 🚌 to the Degollada de Peraza *Descend the path at the right of the* mirador. *View over reservoirs in the Barranco de las Lajas (shown on page 28 and the cover); outlook to Tenerife*

23 PLAYA DE LA CALETA (map pages 112-113) 🌲

by car only: 5-10min on foot
🚗 at the beach. Take the Playa de Hermigua road, north of the DISA petrol station in Hermigua, followed by the first right turn, swinging back up the valley. Then turn left uphill on a road sign-posted for Playa la Caleta. At the top of the crest keep left again for the beach. Car tour 6 *A pretty, remote beach, with full zona recreativa facilities and a small bar/restaurant. Don't swim here unless the sea is dead calm!*

25a AGULO (map pages 120-121, photograph page 119) ○

by car: 15-20min on foot
by bus: 15-20min on foot
🚗 Parking area off the main road outside Agulo. Car tour 6. 🚌 to Agulo
Follow Walk 25 (page 119) to climb the trail just above the cemetery. Sit on the steps above the garden plots. Glorious seascape, with El Teide just across the sea. The only shade is near the cemetery.

25b ROSA DE LAS PIEDRAS (map pages 120-121)

by car only: up to 5min on foot
🚗 Rosa de las Piedras. Detour on Car tour 6
Picnic at the mirador *overlooking the Vallehermoso countryside. Shade*

26 LA MESETA (map page 127, photograph page 124)

by car only: up to 30min on foot
🚗 Park at the entrance to the Camino Forestal de la Meseta, east of the restaurant Chorros de Epina. Car tour 6
Walk along the forestry track and enjoy the pretty barrancos *and far-reaching views. You could also take Short walk 26 described on page 123 to the Presa de los Gallos.*

La Gomera's *zonas recreativas*

(See touring map of La Gomera for 🌲-symbol. All have shade, tables, benches, water; see appropriate car tour for description.)

ERMITA DE LAS NIEVES (Car tour 5) Barbecues

LA PALMITA (near Car tour 6) Barbecues

EL CEDRO (Car tour 5)

CHORROS DE EPINA (Car tour 6)

JARDIN DE LAS CRECES (Car tour 6) Barbecues

RASO DE LA BRUMA (Car tour 6)

MERIGA (Car tour 6, beyond the Juego de Bolas) *No* water

LAGUNA GRANDE (Car tours 5 and 6) Barbecues, toilets, play area, bar/restaurant

✿ Touring

Most people holidaying on Tenerife and Gomera hire a car for some part of their stay. It's very easy to travel between the islands — just 50 minutes by fast ferry (see timetables on page 133).

The four relatively long tours described here will get you well acquainted with **Tenerife**. If your time is limited, **Tour 1 is a must**, with **Tour 4** making a good follow-up.

There are two itineraries for **La Gomera**: I've simply split the island north/south. Should you only be visiting Gomera for one day, you can combine the two tours, *if you make a very early start* by fast ferry from Los Cristianos on Tenerife. If you're spending more time on Gomera and you're hiring a 4WD vehicle, you may find it helpful to use the *walking maps* for touring, since only a few *tracks* are shown on the touring map.

The touring notes are brief: they contain little history or information readily available in leaflets freely available from the tourist offices. The facilities and 'sights' of the main towns are not described either, for the same reason. Instead, I concentrate on the 'logistics' of touring: times and distances, road conditions, and seeing places many tourists miss. Most of all, I emphasise possibilities for **walking** and **picnicking**. While some of the references to picnics 'off the beaten track' (indicated by the symbol *P* in the touring notes) may not be suitable during a long car tour, you may see a landscape that you would like to explore another day.

The large fold-out touring maps are designed to be held out opposite the touring notes and contain all the information you will need outside the towns. The tours have been written up starting from Playa de las Américas (Tenerife) and Valle Gran Rey (La Gomera), but they can be joined from other points quite easily. Town plans are on the touring map.

Remember to allow plenty of time for **visits**, and to take along **warm clothing** as well as some **food and drink**, in case you are delayed. The distances quoted in the notes are *cumulative* from the departure point. A key to the symbols is on the touring maps.

All motorists should read the Country code on page 40. *Buen viaje!*

Tour 1: LAS CAÑADAS AND THE NORTHWEST

Playa de las Américas • Vilaflor • Las Cañadas • La Orotava • Puerto de la Cruz • Icod de los Vinos • Buenavista • Punta de Teno • Masca • Santiago del Teide • Los Gigantes • San Juan • Playa de las Américas

240km/149mi; 8-9 hours' driving; Exit A from Playa de las Américas (plan on reverse of touring map)
En route: ⊞ at La Caldera, Las Lajas, Las Cañadas; Picnics (see **P** *symbol and pages 130-131): (4), 5-8; Walks 2, (3, 4), 5-8. (Other walks and secluded picnic spots are described in* Landscapes of Tenerife.*)*
This excursion requires a very early start. You may set off in sunshine, but often the north is under cloud. Less experienced drivers may find the road between Santiago and Masca unnerving. **Important:** *the road to Punta de Teno is dangerous during heavy rain and strong winds, due to rock fall. Puerto and La Orotava, best reached by motor-way, can visited another day. Adeje (Picnic 4 and Walk 4) lies just off the homeward route, but it's easily reached by bus and also best kept for another day. Note that there are no petrol stations en route between Vilaflor and Arafo.*
Opening hours: Aguamansa trout farm: 10.00-15.00 daily; **Botanical Garden, Puerto de la Cruz:** 09.00-19.00 daily (18.00 in winter)

This dramatic circuit begins on the dry rocky slopes of the south. Ascending to Las Cañadas, you head up through a forest of Canary pines — the most beautiful you'll ever see. Las Cañadas is another world; you will cross a vast bare plateau, where rich volcanic hues ooze out of the landscape, and fields of jagged scoria and sunken gravel 'lakes' (*cañadas*) surround you. The north then greets you with the greenery of garden plots and trees; the lush Orotava Valley is a sea of rippling banana palms. Exhilarating coastal scenery takes you to the northwest and its concealed valleys. From gentle, scooped-out basins, you will plunge into precipitous, fathomless ravines.

Looking down to the Barranco de Masca, starting point for Walk 8

Head east along the TF481 (Exit A). At the Los Cristianos junction turn off for Arona and follow the TF28, passing the Camel Park (★). Some 4.5km uphill, turn left on the TF51, passing a road to the Las Aguilas Jungle Park★. You climb through a bleak landscape. Cacti and *tabaiba* flourish in this rocky terrain, and mock pepper trees grow alongside the road. Come into **Arona** (11km ♦️✕ ⏹️ 📷), where Walk 2 begins and ends. The village has a charming shady church square, surrounded by balconied old houses. Hillocks of all shapes and sizes disrupt the plains.

Continue on the TF51 towards Vilaflor. Vineyards on walled slopes border the road as you rise up to **Vilaflor** (25km ♦️▲▲▲ ✕⏹️⊕📷M), the highest town on the island (1161m/3810ft). Nestled on the edge of a plain, this mountain settlement looks up onto the steep forested inclines that run down off the high mountain spurs above. From Vilaflor follow the TF21 north, passing some of Tenerife's loveliest Canarian pine forests. **Pino Gordo**, a *mirador* 2km past Vilaflor, sits amidst these regal ancient pines (📷). Leaving the viewpoint, at Lomo Blanco you pass the track where Walk 6 can end. Then the road climbs through spectacular rugged mountain landscapes, passing the **Las Lajas** *zona recreativa* 36km ⴰ).

You enter **Las Cañadas★** at the pass of **Boca Tauce** (42km P5), where Walk 5 begins and ends. The twisted uprising of rock over to the left here is more impressive when approached from this direction. A spellbinding lunar landscape unfolds before you. The constant change of colour and rock formation within the encircling crater walls is the highlight of this tour and, I imagine, of your visit. Sharp-surfaced lava flows give way to smooth mounds of scoria, while sunken gravel beds create 'pools' along the floor. Majestic El Teide is with you wherever you go, always more impressive from a distance.

Heading right at the pass, you first skirt the immense gravel plain called **Llano de Ucanca**, almost immediately passing its eponymous *mirador* (📷). Further along, intriguing bright patches of blue and green rock in the roadside embankment catch your attention — **Los Azulejos** (The Tiles). Stop a while at the **Parador de las Cañadas** (49km ▲▲✕i), where Walk 6 begins, to explore the **Piedras Amarillas** (Yellow Stones; *P*6) and the **Roques de García** on the opposite side of the road. These strange rocky upthrusts, the most famous of which is shown opposite, stand guard over the eastern edge of the Ucanca Plain.

Pass by the turn-off to the Teide funicular (you would waste most of the day queueing here) and continue via the **Tabonal** and **Minas de San José** viewpoints (📷) to the **Cañadas Visitors' Centre** (i wc). This is an excellent source of information on the national park, with a small museum and an hourly film show. While the park covers more than 720 sq km, its focal point is a huge crater with a diameter of almost 16km (10mi). In spring you may see the exquisite, 2m/7ft-tall *taginaste rojo* flowering here — a magnificent sight when its tapering stem is embellished with bright red florets. Immediately beyond the visitors' centre is **El Portillo**

(64km ✕⚏wc), the 'Little Gateway'.

From here head left, descending through pines. Soon there are views over the verdant north to Puerto de la Cruz and the built-up coastline. Keep an eye out for the **Mirador Piedra la Rosa★** (74km ⚏), a viewpoint over a rock formation resembling a rose. You'll pass several roadside picnic areas on this road, before you come to the signposted turn-off to **La Caldera★** (81km ✕⚏wc). From this little crater (*caldera*), there are wonderful views over the green slopes of La Orotava and the sea. Just below the La Caldera turn-off lies the **Aguamansa trout farm** (82km ⚏wc and ❀). From there lovely countryside scenery of tilled plots amongst sagging, lichen-covered walls and scatterings of aged chestnut trees takes you down to **La Orotava★** (95km ⚶▲✕⚏⊕M), known for its Corpus Christi festival (May/June).

Continue on the TF21 down to Puerto. If you're interested in botany (especially island flora), you might stop at the **Botanical Garden** (❀). The compact garden is well laid out and contains a substantial collection of tropical and subtropical plants. It's on your route, some 2km south of Puerto, in the suburb of La Paz.

Puerto de la Cruz★ (103km ⚶▲✕⚏⊕⚏Mwc), once a small port serving the farming town of La Orotava, is a bubbly, rather pleasant resort — as resorts go. What little remains of the old town lies buried amidst hotels and apartment blocks. You may wish to visit the 17th-century remains of the old port's heritage: the church of Nuestra Señora de la Peña, the Chapel of San Telmo and the Castillo de San Felipe (now a restaurant). The Casa Iriarte, a charming 18th-century house, is considered to be the best example of Canarian architecture in Puerto.

From Puerto take the motorway west towards San Juan de la Rambla, continuing on the TF320 when it ends. The coastal road passes below cliffs towering up to the left, while breakers crash below on the right (113km ⚏⚏ **Mirador de San Pedro**; 116km ⚏ **Barranco de Ruiz**). **San Juan de la Rambla** (119km ✕⚏) is a charming, fresh-white village overlooking the sea. Las Aguas, a neighbouring village on the rocky shoreline below, is a picture-postcard scene glimpsed just before San Juan. All the way from Puerto to the northwestern tip of the island, you're immersed in banana palms and bright seasonal blooms.

Roque Cinchado, the most dramatic of the Roques de García, has been incorrectly (but understandably) known as 'God's Finger' for years.

The famous dragon tree at Icod de los Vinos

Continuing along the TF320, come into **Icod de los Vinos**★ (129km 🚻🏨🏦🍴🚌⊕) on the fertile, vine-growing slopes below El Teide. The Church of San Marcos (16/17C) is worth a visit. Just below the church square is Icod's famous ancient dragon tree ... and the 'Butterfly House'. Nearby Playa de San Marcos, a resort that never took off, is a small sandy beach surrounded by dark and jagged cliffs (a 5km return detour). Manorial homes amidst banana plantations come into view as you leave Icod on the TF42, soon hugging the coast. Come into **Garachico**★ (135km 🚻🏨🏦🍴🚌⊕M). This beautifully-situated village, once an important port, was destroyed by a volcanic eruption in the early 18th century. But a few buildings of interest survive: the 16th-century San Miguel Castle, the Baroque palace of the Marqués de Adeje and the 17th-century Convent of San Francisco, and the Church of Santa Ana (founded in 1548). Garachico is also known for its inviting natural rock pools. The Roque de Garachico, rising off the shore, bears a cross to protect the site from another catastrophe.

Continuing west on the TF42 you pass through the narrow streets of **Los Silos** (141km 🚻🚌🪑). Further along this coastal plain lies **Buenavista** (145km 🍴🚌⊕🪑). The village is walled in by high sharp crags; gorges and valleys cut back into this cataclysm of rock. Just past the Plaza de San Sebastián, where there is a small chapel on the right, turn left, following signs for Punta de Teno. Some 5km along the TF445, there are especially fine views from the **Punta del Fraile** (📷), where the island falls away into an indigo sea. The road wind round and under rough indented cliffs, high above the sea, and then descends to the lighthouse on the dark volcanic promontory of **Punta de Teno** (155km 📷), one of the richest botanical areas in the Canaries. Swimming off the rocks in the crystal clear water here is a must!

Revived, return to Buenavista (164km) and, at the junction, turn right on the TF436 for El Palmar. A steep climb through rocky terrain covered in prickly pear, *vinagrera, verode, tabaiba* and wild geraniums lead you up to El Palmar's lush valley, hidden far above the coastal plain. The reclining valley walls — a mass of thin green lines — are terraced straight up to the crests. Pass through **El Palmar** (170km) and, 1km further on, turn right on the narrow country lane signposted to Teno Alto. A steep climb (☐) takes you up to **Teno Alto** (178km ✕☐) — a tiny outpost of farms scattered across a tableland amidst scrub and pastures. Try the simple home cooking in the restaurant here, especially the *cabrito* (kid) and *garbanzos* (chickpeas) … and don't miss the wine.

Then return to the El Palmar road and head right. At the highest point on the road, pause at the pass of **La Tabaiba** (190km ☐) to take in the dramatic difference between the El Palmar and Masca valleys — the former smooth and sweeping, the latter sharp and turbulent. Then wind downhill into deep gorges, where various *miradors* (☐) open up magnificent views — especially over **Masca** (195km ✕☐*P8*), a favourite village amongst the islanders themselves. Walk 8 descends the spectacular ravine here (photograph page 13), a narrow corridor of 700m-high rock walls that ends at an equally spectacular beach.

Climbing out of the gorges, you pass the starting point for Walk 7 (*P7*; photograph page 65). You cross a pass with far-reaching views to La Gomera, La Palma and El Hierro and then begin the descent, with El Teide making a splendid backdrop. From the sleepy village of **Santiago del Teide** (201km ☨✕☐⊕☐) join the TF82 and turn right towards Los Gigantes. **Tamaimo** (208km ✕☐) is an attractive village sheltering below a high rocky protrusion. From Tamaimo, keep right on the TF454. Greenhouses for tomatoes now cover the landscape, as the route winds down to Los Gigantes.

At a junction (213km), keep right for Puerto de Santiago. **Los Gigantes** (215km ▲▲ ✕☐) is a modern tourist complex, set against a backdrop of sheer cliffs★ rising vertically out of the sea. From Los Gigantes make for nearby **Puerto de Santiago** (▲▲✕ ☐⊕) and the adjoining Playa de la Arena. Continue past **Alcalá** (▲✕☐) to tranquil **San Juan** (225km ▲▲✕☐). Keeping straight on along the coast, you briefly rejoin the TF82 just below Adeje (Walks 3 and 4), before picking up the motorway to return to **Playa de las Américas** (240km).

Los Cristianos

Tour 2: THE CUMBRE AND THE SUN-BAKED SOUTH

Playa de las Américas • Guía de Isora • Las Cañadas • El Portillo • Güimar • Arico • Granadilla • Playa de las Américas

212km/131mi; about 5-6 hours' driving; Exit B from Playa de las Américas (plan on reverse of touring map)
En route: 戸 at Chio, Las Cañadas, Monte Los Frailes; Picnics (see *P* symbol and pages 130-131): 5, 6; Walks: (3, 4), 5, 6 (Other walks and secluded

picnic spots are described in *Landscapes of Tenerife*.)
Driving is generally good, except for some 30km of bumpy narrow road along the TF28. The cumbre above Arafo is often shrouded in low-lying mists. Note that there are no petrol stations en route between

From the greenest to the driest, from the lowest to the highest, this drive has it all. The higher inclines along the southern flanks of the island, missed by most tourists, are a dramatic contrast to the rich green slopes of the north.

Set off from Exit B in Playa de las Américas, heading north, first along the motorway, then the TF82, making for Guía de Isora. The road gradually ascends, passing below Adeje (Walks 3 and 4), cutting through rocky ridges and dipping into *barrancos*. There are uninterrupted views along a coastline robed in banana palms. **Guía de Isora** (19km ✗🏠⊕) is a small country town sitting high on the bare rocky slopes. It's worth wandering around the narrow streets here, before setting off again.

Coming into **Chio** (23km 🏠), turn right on the TF38 for Las Cañadas. Las Estrellas restaurant (✗🖼), not far along, is a fine viewing point over the southwest coast. Pines begin appearing, scattered across the landscape, and smooth volcanic cones remind you of the most recent volcanic outbursts. Set amidst this scenery is the lovely **Chio** *zona recreativa* (戸). The pines subside, and dark lava flows spill across the landscape. **Narices del Teide** (50km 🖼), a *mirador* at the foot of the prominent Pico Viejo on your left, allows you to pull over to enjoy this intriguing sight.

You enter **Las Cañadas**★ at the pass of **Boca Tauce** (53km *P*5, Walk 5): continue on the TF21 along the crater floor, with the towering wall of peaks rising impressively alongside you. El Teide dominates the landscape, but Guajara (Tenerife's third highest mountain; photograph page 58, top) projects noticeably out of the crater walls. The route from Boca Tauce is described in Car tour 1: use the notes on page 14 as far as **El Portillo** (75km).

At El Portillo turn off right on the TF24 to climb the *cumbre*. Anthill-sized cones grow out of the inclines below the road. *Retama* (a hardy yellow-flowering broom), white-blooming *margarita del Teide* (of the daisy family), and mauve-flowering *alhelí del Teide* creep across the terrain. The tones in the gravel slopes change from maroon, purple and black to grey, mauve and russet. **La Crucita** (90km 🖼; photograph opposite) is the point where pilgrims cross the TF24 on their way from the north to Candelaria for the celebration of the Assumption of the Virgin of Candelaria, Tenerife's patron saint.

Pines reappear and the countryside becomes rockier and rougher. You snatch far-reaching views along the way from a series of viewpoints. A detour of 1km takes you to the **Mirador de Cumbres** (), which looks out over the pine-wooded northern slopes to El Teide. **Mirador de Ortuño** () follows; it offers similar views. Finally, you come to the **Mirador Pico de las Flores** (111km). This viewpoint looks out over the verdant hills of La Esperanza, all the way to Santa Cruz and up to the Anaga range.

From Mirador Pico de las Flores retrace your route for 13km, then turn left on the TF523, to descend to the sun-bleached south via Arafo and Güimar. Pines give way to loose scatterings of chestnuts, which cover the lower slopes (at **Monte Los Frailes**). The Güimar basin opens up ahead, revealing great ravines cutting back deep into

El Teide dominates the skyline at the pass of La Crucita.

the steep escarpment. High brown stone terraces step the slopes of this productive agricultural centre. Vineyards interspersed with vegetable patches cover the greater part of the land. Bypassing the centre of Arafo, go straight through **Güimar★** (145km ⛰✕🍴⊕M and 'Pirámides de Güimar' 🎦). Keep to the left of the church, then turn right along the *avenida*. At the T-junction turn right on the TF28 for Fasnia.

This bumpy old road winds in and out of shallow ravines before climbing out of the basin along the eastern escarpment, from where you have a superb view over the valley and towards the Anaga Peninsula. From here on, the monotone landscape is more harsh. Trees have vanished, save for the fine-branched Jerusalem thorn bordering the roadside. In April and November its blossoms cheer up this countryside. Rock walls terrace the slopes.

Fasnia (162km 🍴⊕) is a pleasant country village set back off the road. Between here and Arico, there are few settlements, and the land looks almost abandoned. Keeping straight on through **Arico** (176km ✕🍴⊕), you eventually come to **Granadilla** (183km ⛲✕🍴⊕), where cultivation returns to the the countryside. This important agricultural centre occupies one of the most fertile valleys in the south and boasts the best oranges on the island. Leaving the town, keep down to the left and follow the TF64 to the motorway, then head right to **Playa de las Américas** (212km).

Tour 3: QUIET CORNERS OF THE NORTHEAST

Playa de las Américas • Tacoronte • Bajamar • Punta del Hidalgo • Cruz del Carmen • Las Carboneras • Taborno • Pico del Inglés • La Laguna • Playa de las Américas

Reckon on 271km/168mi; 5-6 hours' driving; Exit A from Playa de las Américas (plan on reverse of touring map)
En route: All the walks and secluded picnic spots along this tour are described and illustrated in Landscapes of Tenerife, which

explores the Anaga Peninsula in detail.
Some 90min of this drive are spent on the motorway, getting to and from the northeast. Because of the narrow and winding roads on the Anaga Peninsula, driving will be slow.

This short excursion visits varied landscapes. You'll drive down to the coast and take a dip in sea-water pools (there are several choices); continue up to the summits of the Anaga and go for a stroll in the laurel forest; then perhaps finish off the day with something of historical and cultural interest, sauntering around the streets of La Laguna.

Take the motorway (Exit A) and head east. **Candelaria★** (61km ✚▲▲✗☎⊕) is a good place for a break, now or on your return. The basilica (1958) houses the new statue of Nuestra Señora de la Candelaria, the island's patron saint. (The original statue, supposedly found in 1390 by Guanche herdsmen, was lost in a tidal wave in 1826.) The large square on the seafront near the modern church is quite impressive, with its red-rock statues representing the ten former Guanche chiefs of Tenerife.

Rejoin the motorway and turn off onto the Autopista del Norte (TF2), which takes you onto the northbound TF5 motorway. Leave the TF5 at the El Sauzal exit (96km), then follow sign-posting to **Tacoronte** (98km ✚▲▲✗☎⊕). The wooden statue of Christ in the 17th-century

church here is revered by many of the islanders and numerous miracles are attributed to it. Immediately past the plaza, turn left on the TF16 and follow it all the way to **Tejina** (108km ✗☎), then join the TF13 for Bajamar. Colourfully blooming bushes and creepers, together with large banana plantations, enliven the landscape along here. The village's tidal pools make the small-scale resort of **Bajamar★** (112km ▲▲▲✗☎⊕) a popular swimming spot. A backdrop of severe rocky ridges and ravines overshadows the settlement, and an abundance of xerophytic plants cling to the dark abrupt inclines.

Continue on the same road to **Punta del Hidalgo★** (115km ▲▲▲△✗☞☎). It lies along a slight bay with a rocky beach, across from Bajamar. The road ends past the village at a round-about, where high craggy crests fall away into the sea.

Return to Tejina, then continue on the TF13 via **Tegueste** (126km ✗☎) to **Las Canteras** (131km ✗☎). Climbing into

20

this village, which straddles a crest, turn sharp left *(blind corner)* onto the TF12. You head up into the magnificent laurel forest. A *mirador* (☞) on the right, 4km from Las Canteras, gives you captivating views of the lush green undulating hills outside La Laguna. One kilometre above the mirador, fork left on the TF143, to make for the isolated village of Batán, hidden in a valley deep in the spine of the peninsula. Keep right all the way downhill. Some 8km of winding road brings you down to **Batán**, superbly sited in stunning mountain scenery. Return from Batán to the TF12 and keep left for **Cruz del Carmen★** (154km ✕☞*i*), a well-designated viewpoint, framed by the forest. From here you overlook the Aguere Valley of La Laguna and have more views of the ever-present Teide.

For a brief time you leave the thick of the forest, as you drive down to two more beautifully-sited villages — Las Carboneras and Taborno: 1km past the turn-off to Pico del Inglés, go left on the TF145. At a fork, keep left for Las Carboneras. Valleys open up as you descend, and Punta del Hidalgo reveals itself for a moment. The Roque de Taborno (photograph above) is a prominent landmark, sitting high atop the ridge. At a further fork again keep left. **Las Carboneras★** (165km ✕) sits glued to a hill, encircled by cultivation.

Now return to the fork passed earlier (TF138) and turn left. After descending a forested ridge, you come into **Taborno★** (170km ☞), where small dwellings are dispersed along the crest of the ridge, rising high above two *barrancos*.

Roque de Taborno: this perfectly-formed spike, often called the 'little Matterhorn', is a prominent feature of the Anaga's landscape of razor-sharp crests.

Return the same way to the main road and turn right. Then head left to **Pico del Inglés★** (179km ☞). Perched on the spine of this range that divides the island north and south, the *mirador* offers views down into the hidden cultivation of the Afur valley, catches snippets of the coast, and looks out to the island's guardian, El Teide. From Pico del Inglés make for **La Laguna★** (191km ♦▲✕☺ ⊕M) on the TF12. There's much to enjoy in this charming university town. Leaving La Laguna, return to the motorway and retrace your outgoing route to **Playa de las Américas** (271km).

Tour 4: BUCOLIC CHARMS OF THE RUGGED ANAGA

Playa de las Américas • Pico del Inglés • Roque Negro • El Bailadero • Chamorga • Taganana • Almáciga • Benijo • San Andrés • Igueste • Santa Cruz • Playa de las Américas

Reckon on 262km/162mi; about 6-7 hours' driving; Exit A from Playa de las Américas (plan on reverse of touring map)
En route: ♒ at the El Bailadero tunnel. (Walks and secluded picnic spots are described in Landscapes of Tenerife, which explores the Anaga in detail.)

Around 1h of the drive is spent on motorways, getting to and from the Anaga. Driving is slow in the mountainous terrain, with fairly heavy tourist traffic. Note: there are no petrol stations between Las Canteras (outskirts of La Laguna) and San Andrés — 83km along the touring route.

This excursion takes us amidst the mountains of the Anaga Peninsula. Twisting along the backbone of this range, the road is one continuous *mirador*. Inland, lost in these rugged contours, lie tiny remote villages, clinging to rocky nodules and buried in *barrancos*. And along the coast, quiet and secluded little bays unravel.

Start out as in Tour 3 (page 20), but shortly after joining the TF5, leave it again: follow signs for Las Canteras/Punta del Hidalgo (TF113). At **Las Canteras** (80km) head right on the TF12, soon immersing yourself in the coolness of the laurel forest and passing the **Mirador Cruz del Carmen** (☜✕*i*).

A kilometre further on, turn right for **Pico del Inglés★** (88km ☜), a fabulous *mirador* with far-reaching views. Head back to the main road (TF12) and turn right. Solitary houses speckle the ridges segmenting the isolated Afur Valley. Some 3km along, turn left on the TF136 for **Roque Negro** (96km ☜), a small, well-concealed settlement over-shadowed by an enormous black basalt rock. The village square serves as a good look-out point: Afur can be seen far below in the shadows of these high crests, and a wild beach, the Playa del Tama-dite, lies beyond the village. (I highly recommend a 4km detour to Afur, just to experience the friendly bar.)

The main tour returns from Roque Negro to the TF12 and heads left. Ravines clothed in subtle shades of green slip off the southern slopes (104km ☜♒). At the 107km-mark, turn off left for **El Bailadero★** (☜✕), the viewpoint from where the photograph opposite was taken. From here on the road is flanked by dense laurel woods. Some 5km further on, you come to the lovely **Anaga Forestry Park**. At the **Mirador de las Chamu-cadas** (113km ☜), you'll have good views down over Igueste, a seaside village built across the mouth of a *barranco* (visited later in the tour).

Descending in S-bends into open rocky terrain, you pass a turn-off right (117km) to Las Bodegas, a hamlet sheltering in a narrow *barranco*. La Cumbrilla is the village perched high on the ridge under which the road passes. **Chamorga** (✕), the most isolated village on Tenerife, lies at the end of the road, a couple of kilometres further on. A smattering of white dwellings, the hamlet snuggles into the sides of a *barranco*, shaded by palms and loquat trees.

22

The stepped valleys of Taganana, from the Mirador El Bailadero

From Chamorga return to the Taganana turn-off (left, just below El Bailadero). Some 2km further down, turn left again (☍). After passing through a tunnel under the Bailadero *mirador*, you overlook a landscape of razor-sharp ridges cutting down to the sea.
Taganana★ (139km ⛺⛽✖⊕), a brilliant array of white houses, is spread across the tumbling lower crests of the valley. Palms and colourful gardens make this settlement extremely photogenic. Roque de las Animas (the Ghosts' Rock), towers straight above the road a kilometre beyond the village.
Roque de las Bodegas (141km ✖) with its roadside restaurant, is a busy tourist stop. Past **Almáciga**, **Benijo** (144km ✖☕), where the tar ends, is just a few cottages high above a beach. But Restaurant El Frontón, with good food and magnificent views, is a pleasant place to take a break.
Retracing your route through the tunnel, follow the TF12 down the Barranco de San Andrés to the south coast. At **San Andrés** (163km ⛺✖⛽), turn left for Igueste. The palms of Las Teresitas (Tenerife's only golden-sand beach) add a touch of the tropics, and the unofficial naturist beach of Las Gaviotes is glimpsed far below, at the foot of the cliffs. Picturesque **Igueste** (171km ✖) sits at the end of this cliff-hugging coastal road. From Igueste follow the coast road all the way to **Santa Cruz** (185km ⛺⛽⛺✖⛽⊕). Make sure you pass through the city before (or well after) the rush hour! Then take the motorway (⛽) back to **Playa de las Américas** (262km).

Walkers' signposting on the Anaga Peninsula; see comments on page 36.

Tour 5: LA GOMERA'S SOUTHERN LANDSCAPES

Valle Gran Rey • Arure • Las Hayas • Chipude • Alajeró • Playa de Santiago • San Sebastián • El Cedro • Los Roques • Laguna Grande • Valle Gran Rey

Reckon on 142km/88mi, 5-6 hours' driving. Join the tour at San Sebastián (page 28) if you come from Tenerife by car ferry.
*En route: ⌂ at the Ermita de las Nieves, El Cedro, Laguna Grande; Picnics (see **P** symbol and pages 10-11): 9, 10, 12, 14-19; Walks: 9-24*
This is a long drive, with several interesting stops en route. An early start is recommended. The roads in the south are good, but the link road between the GM1 and GM2,
which serves El Cedro and Los Roques, is often closed due to landslips. If so, visit this area on foot (Short walk 15-1, Shorter walk 18, and Walk 19). The narrow cobbled road to El Cedro may be unnerving for some motorists. Always be alert for foraging goats and sheep on the roads — and, around settlements, for pedestrians. Note that petrol stations en route are few and far between and that their opening hours on Sundays and holidays may be restricted!

Y ou will be astonished at what this island of 378 square miles has to offer! This tour introduces you to the south of La Gomera, which at first glance appears bare, barren and sun-baked. For most tourists, perhaps it is. But *you* will find valley floors laden with produce, grassy saucer-shaped basins, elegant palm groves and pockets of pines. The out-of-the-way beaches (stony in winter, sandy in summer) will entice you to return for a 'beach day'. Heading back to Valle Gran Rey, you enter another world — a salubrious forest, dark and damp and dripping with moss. Short walks, perhaps to picnic spots, lead you through this relic of the Tertiary Period, to fern-drenched slopes and cascading streams. You needn't be a walker to enjoy this rare gift of nature, but you may become one!

Leaving Valle Gran Rey, a dramatic climb takes you up the sheer walls of the Gran Rey *barranco* — the island's most picturesque valley (**P9**; Walks 9 and 10). You look out over a verdant tapestry of palm and banana groves, gardens, and a stream bed filled with cane. Several *miradors* allow you to pull over and enjoy different corners of the valley. But the one not to miss is the **Mirador El Palmarejo** (8.5km 📷✕), which sits high in the escarpment at the northern end of the valley. Designed by the late César Manrique, the beauty of this

unobtrusive viewpoint lies in the simplicity of design and decor — as with all his creations in his native Lanzarote.
Rounding the sheer walls of the Barranco de Arure (an adjoining valley), you soon pass the bar/restaurant El Jape in **Arure**, the starting point for Walks 11 and 12, as well as Shorter walk 10. Just around the bend you will come to your turn-off right for Las Hayas (10km). But if this is the only tour you will be taking on La Gomera, first *turn left* at this junction and go on for about 200m to a lane signposted left for the **Mirador Ermita del**

Santo (🏛♨*P*10). Some 300m along the lane, just beyond the path to the *mirador,* you'll find a parking area. This very dramatic viewpoint overlooks the isolated Taguluche Valley and the village of Taguluche some 500m/1650ft below. Return to the Las Hayas fork and head left.

The main tour keeps right at the Las Hayas fork. The road passes above an enchanting reservoir and climbs to the plateau, where you meander across an undulating tableland that rises up into the centre of the island. The islands of La Palma (with the twin 'humps') and El Hierro can be seen not too far in the distance. La Fortaleza (Walk and Picnic 14), the prominent buttress of rock up ahead, soon steals your attention. Coming into palm trees, enter **Las Hayas** (15.5km ✕*P*12). Vegetarians may like to eat at La Montaña, where Doña Efigenia has been serving up the same local meal for decades. She's become quite famous — the place is mostly visited by tourists. If you decide to combine lunch here with Short walk 12-2 or Alternative walk 26, *be prepared for slow service and bring a jacket — the restaurant is not heated.*

Leaving the village, you come to a junction at the edge of the laurel forest. Turn right for **El Cercado** (20km ✕), the centre for ceramics. This charming village, characterised by its rustic stone cottages, sits around a cultivated basin cut up into small vegetable gardens. You look across a hillside heavily lined with stone walls on the approach to **Chipude** (24.5km ♨✕🏛). Short walk 13 (quite an easy walk and *highly recommended for all visitors*) begins here, at the church square. (Walk 14 also passes through Chipude, and

Walk 15 ends here.) Just outside the village, pass the turn-off for La Dama; if you need petrol, go right here; Chipude's petrol station is 0.3km down this turn-off. La Fortaleza now dominates the landscape with its massive crown of rock. Pines merge into the surrounding cloak of heather. The **Mirador de Igualero** (29km ♨🎦) gives you a chance to pull over and admire La Fortaleza in all its grandeur. Erquito is the sprinkling of houses in the *barranco* floor far below.

A short way further on, turn right for Alajeró and begin a drawn-out descent to Playa de Santiago. The countryside is bare of trees and heavily smudged with rock. You peer down into sheer-sided ravines that appear without warning. Elevated tongues of land dip towards the sea, terminating abruptly in cliffs. Luminous green *tabaiba* enlivens the sombre hillsides. Four kilometres downhill you pass the **Mirador del Drago** (🎦), from where there is a fine view over the harsh countryside. To see the dragon tree for which the *mirador* is named involves a 20-minute descent down a steep cobbled trail into the valley below and another 35 minutes to climb back up! Unfortunately, you can't get too close either — it's been fenced off.

One kilometre beyond the *mirador* you come to the turn-off left for Imada. The main tour continues straight ahead here but, were you to drive 0.6km along the road towards Imada, you would have a truly magnificent view over that village and its dramatic setting. Unfortunately, there is no lay-by, the road is very narrow, and the best view is from a bend in the road! If you take this short detour, *please be on the alert for other traffic.*

Palms, dotting the inclines, announce the scattered village of **Alajeró** (37.5km ☗). Take the first turning right, down to the church square. To get back to the main road, take the first left turn just below the church. But first, if you'd like to stretch your legs, you could park in Alajeró and take a short walk (1h return) to the Ermita San Isidro on **Calvario**, a peak to the south-west. To get there, turn left below the church (as for the car tour), go left at the next cross-roads and then, after 100m/yds, take the street to the right (refer to the map on page 96). At the next fork (10 minutes from the church), go right to the foot of the peak, from where a paved path leads to the summit with its fine view towards La Fortaleza and Garajonay.

Beyond Alajeró you're soon looking across to Tenerife, made bold by the prominence of El Teide; this magnificent sight will remain with you all the way to San Sebastián. Two picturesque hamlets — Targa and then Antoncojo — huddled up against rocky outcrops on your left may catch your attention as you descend through this dusty, thirsty landscape. The turn-off for Targa (Walk 16; *P*16) is passed at 40km and later the island's tiny airport — the most beautiful in the Canaries, but with hardly any flights, since the ferry connections from Tenerife are so good.

Banana plantations sitting back off the sea-cliffs betray **Playa de Santiago** (51km ⛰▲✕🏢⊕) below, at the confluence of two large ravines. As you approach down the most westerly of the ravines, keep right for the port. This once-quiet fishing village has grown rapidly, with apartments and timeshares taking advantage of the best weather on the island, and little shops and restaurants strung out along the waterfront to cater for tourists. Turn left at the seafront. Just before the road begins to climb out of the second *barranco* (Barranco de Santiago), you could take a 5km return detour up the east side of the *barranco:* take the next road off left, signposted for Pastrana. Non-walkers might especially enjoy this drive, to see the tucked-away hamlets of Taco, El Rumbazo (Walk 16) and Pastrana (Walk 18; *P18*). These three humble settlements sit in the shadows of towering jagged walls, overlooking a valley floor crammed with gardens and

The aptly-named peak of El Sombrero, not far below the Degollada de Peraza

orchards. This oasis of greenery is the last thing you would expect to see when you enter this initially inhospitable-looking gorge. Pastrana also houses a friendly little restaurant with outdoor terrace, serving local specialties in a beautiful setting (closed Mondays).

The main tour bypasses this turn-off and, on reaching the main road, heads right, zig-zagging up out of the Barranco de Santiago past banana groves, vineyards and avocado plots. This is the domain of Fred Olsen, the Norwegian shipping magnate, who developed the large Jardín Tecina Hotel, the golf course above it and the Pueblo Don Tomas urbani-sation. Steadily climbing, you enter a landscape carved up by more impressive ravines, separated by razor-sharp ridges flecked with *tabaiba*. Pockets of palms occupy corners of the

barrancos. Further inland, pines, splashed in amongst *Cistus* and prickly pear, add more hues to the greenery.

Some 14km from Playa de Santiago you come to a junction at the **Degollada de Peraza** (65.5km ✕ ⌕*P19*; Walks 19 and 20). Stop at the *mirador* and look at the clean-cut Las Lajas Valley and its delightfully-stepped reservoirs (photograph page 28 and cover). Walk 19 would take you high up this appealing gorge. There's also another short detour possible from this pass: you could follow the Hermigua road to the left for 1km and then take the first right turn you come to. This leads to the lovely Ermita de las Nieves *zona recreativa* (⌗♦), with all facilities.

The main tour keeps *right* at the pass, to continue through a landscape littered with stone walls. The ridges no longer burst

up angrily out of the valleys. El Sombrero, a hat-shaped rock adorning a parallel ridge, steals your attention five minutes down (photograph pages 26-27). Then the verdure in the hillsides slowly fades, and the landscape becomes barren and sun-baked once more.

San Sebastián (82.5km ♦♠♠ ✕🍴⊕M; Walk 21) is a charming little town with some lovely pedestrian areas and plenty of small bars where you can enjoy a drink or a coffee. For those in search of history, there's the Church of the Assumption, where Columbus supposedly attended mass before setting off on his historic journey to the New World; also Columbus's house (Casa de Colón) and the simply-built Torre del Conde (Count's Tower, a 500-year-old fortress built by Felipe II). The last now houses a small museum with artefacts from La Gomera and South America, dating back to the period before the Spanish Conquest.

Leaving the town, follow signs for Hermigua. The wide valley floor closes up into a narrow V. Sharply-outlined ridges run down off the *barranco* walls. Closer to the *cumbre*, the craggy slopes are greener. Keep an eye open for the large clumps of candelabra spurge on the inclines above. Some 8km from San Sebastián, you pass the Camino Forestal de Majona on the right, where Walk 22 begins and Walk 23 ends. And from this northbound road you have an even better view over the reservoirs in the Barranco de las Lajas. In winter the valley comes to life, when the streams are full, and water cascades over the reservoir walls. The road curls its way up the *barranco*, in and out of tunnels. Scarred cliffs tower above. Leaving the south behind, you pass the Los Cumbres restaurant (✕) and soon duck into a long tunnel. Emerging on the north side of the island, a completely different landscape confronts you: heather and strands of laurel forest cap the summits and trail down the upper inclines. Sheer dome-shaped peaks stand shoulder-to-shoulder over on the right. A parking place (📷) beside a white abandoned house a few hundred metres beyond the tunnel exit enables you to pull over and enjoy this sudden change of scene. You get a taste of the north — of Car tour 6. Your views encompass the banana plantations of Hermigua below.

One kilometre further on

The Izcagüe and Chejelipes reservoirs in the Barranco de las Lajas

(97km), turn left for El Cedro and head up into the **Garajonay National Park★**. This amazing, well-engineered road snakes up the precipitous wooded slopes of the *cumbre*. Springs trickle down out of the mossy banks. House-leeks of different shapes and sizes speckle the rock faces and white-to-carmine-coloured flowers (*Senecio*) fleck the shady banks. Lichen-clad heather and moss-covered laurels shade the route. The air is damp; for much of the year, the *cumbre* lies shrouded in mist, which has a special beauty all its own. The *miradors* of **El Rejo** (☎) and **El Bailadero** (☎) will more than likely be in cloud.

Soon (103km) you come to the signposted turn-off for the hamlet of El Cedro. Don't miss this scenic spot! Midway down this cobbled forestry road you will come to a fork: a left leads into the centre of the forest (to the Las Mimbreras parking area), a right takes you down to **El Cedro★** (✖⚷), where the only parking is at the restaurant La Vista. You really need half a day to explore the hamlet and the enchanting forest with its picnic area on foot: see notes for Walk 15 (page 86) and Walk 24 (page 115).

Returning from El Cedro, you mount the crest of the *cumbre* and soon reach a junction, the **Cruce de la Zarcita** (111km), where Walk 15 begins. Turn left here. After about 0.5km you come to one of the island's most famous viewpoints — **Los Roques★** (☎). It's an intriguing place, where four enormous pillars of lava (the remains of volcanic chimneys) burst up out of the landscape. The two viewing platforms on the right overlook Roque de Agando, a massive protrusion growing

straight up out of the sweeping Barranco de Benchijigua. El Teide rises in the background, beyond the finely-etched ravines of La Villa and Las Lajas. Another balcony, on the left-hand side of the road, looks out onto the stouter rocks of Ojila, Zarcita and Carmen (from left to right). A fourth *mirador* lies just below these two. Shorter walk 18 begins here.

Return to Cruce de la Zarcita and turn left. Shortly after you remount the *cumbre,* be sure to pull over at the **Mirador de Tajaque** (☎) and take in the panorama over the immense Barranco de Benchijigua on the south side of the ridge (Walk 18; photograph page 94). Just 100m short of the KM22 road marker, you pass a signposted track junction to the left of the road, near the **Caseta de los Noruegos** (*P*17). At the **Pajarito round-about** (116.5km; *P*15), where Walk 17 begins, keep right towards Laguna Grande. You could climb to Garajonay's summit from here (Alternative walk 17), but an easier ascent begins 1km further on, at **Alto del Contadero** (Short walk 15-2). A strip of pine trees runs down off the mountain, fraying out as it enters the heath-tree vegetation zone.

Pass the **Laguna Grande** picnic area (120km ✖⚷) and, at the next junction (Cruce de las Hayas) head left. Then take the first right to **Las Hayas** (✖). From here follow your outgoing route to return to **Valle Gran Rey** (142km). Descending into this grand valley at sunset, you find the *barranco* in another mood: its austere façade is softer, and the walls no longer frown down upon you. If you haven't fallen in love with La Gomera by now, you never will.

Tour 6: LA GOMERA'S VERDANT NORTH

Valle Gran Rey • Las Hayas • Laguna Grande • Hermigua • Agulo • Garajonay National Park Visitors' Centre • Vallehermoso • Arure • Valle Gran Rey

102km/63mi; 4-5 hours' driving. If you come from Tenerife by car ferry, join (and leave) the tour at the El Rejo junction: head north up the GM1 and pick up the notes at the 36km-point (page 31).
En route: ⌐ at Chorros de Epina, Laguna Grande, (Mériga, Jardín de las Creces and Raso de la Bruma are not far away); Picnics (see P symbol and pages 130-133): 9, 10, 12, 15, 17, 23, 25, 26; Walks 9-12, 15, 17, 19, 23-27
The roads are winding, and there are some rough patches: driving will be slow. The link road between the GM1 and GM2, which serves El Cedro and Los Roques, is often closed due to landslips. If so, visit this area on foot (Short walk 15-1, Shorter walk 18, and Walk 19). Watch out for foraging goats and sheep on the roads, and for pedestrians in the villages. There are only three petrol stations en route: at Valle Gran Rey, Hermigua and Vallehermoso; note that on Sundays and holidays their opening times may be restricted.

The perfect way to begin this drive is to catch a sunrise from atop Garajonay. The majestic beauty of El Teide, in rapidly changing hues of gold, orange and mauve, afloat on a sea of white clouds, is a sight you'll long remember. But if you're not an early bird, the sunset is often equally rewarding. On this tour you delve into the rugged north, where narrow ravines carve up the countryside. The hillsides, patched in scrub and capped with woods, are discernibly greener than in the south. Banana palms, orchards and garden plots fill the stream beds, intensifying the greenery. Tall palms gracefully ornament picturesque villages. But alas, all too frequently a cape of cloud descends before midday — another good reason for an early start.

Follow Car tour 5 as far as the junction just beyond **Las Hayas** (16.5km). Here keep straight on (the left fork) and, when you come to a T-junction, turn right. Crossing the rolling hills of the island's centre, you thread your way through heather and laurel. Pine woods appear in the background. You pass the sunken *zona recreativa* of **Laguna Grande** (21.5km ✕⌐). The restaurant here, with its cosy fireplace, is worth keeping in mind … in case you hit one of the really cold spells that the island sometimes saves up for visitors. A meal here will set you up for any drop in the temperature!
If it's a fine day, you'll want to climb **Garajonay★**, to enjoy the extensive views. The easiest route is from Alto del Contadero, 2.7km beyond Laguna Grande. Pull into the large parking area on your left and climb the signposted track opposite, using the notes on page 86 (Short walk 15-2). It takes about 20 minutes to reach the summit. On the ascent, you will look across pine trees to the imposing rock shown opposite,

La Fortaleza. As the name suggests, the rock resembles a fortress. On clear days, the view from Garajonay (*P*15) encompasses El Hierro, La Palma, Tenerife and Gran Canaria. Continuing the tour towards Hermigua, enjoy more superb views off either side of the *cumbre*, the island's backbone. Keep left at the **Pajarito roundabout** (25km), where Walk 17 and Alternative walk 17 begin. Some 0.7km further on, 100m past the KM22 marker stone, you pass a heavily signposted track junction at the right of the road. A track turns off right here, near the **Caseta de los Noruegos — the 20min-point in Walk 17** (*P*17). Twisting down through the laurel forest, you come to **Cruce de la Zarcita** (29km), starting point for Walk 15. Turn left here to make for the north. (But if you're not doing Tour 5, first continue to the right, to see **Los Roques★** (Short walk 18 and Walk 19), described on page 29.)

Plump peaks, all in a line, rise abruptly up out of the valley over to your right. On route to Hermigua you pass the forestry road to El Cedro (see Car tour 5, page 29), followed by the two *miradors* of **El Bailadero** (📷) and **El Rejo** (📷). At the El Rejo junction (36km), where you join the GM1, turn left. Some 2.7km along, you may wish to take a road off to the left to the Roque de San Pedro, the rock shown on the cover (a detour of about 1km). From there you could follow Walk 24 for 20-30 minutes, to explore the Barranco del Cedro — the lushest gorge on the island. (See page 115 and the map on pages 112-113.)

Hermigua (44km ✝🏔🏠✕🚤⊕ M***P***23) is a striking contrast of white houses and green banana groves. Hamlets step corners of the ravine walls and stretch along the floor. Fruit trees grow amidst the houses. Walk 24 starts and ends here, and Walk 23 begins here. Three places you might like to visit are the Los Telares Museum (a small collection of traditional household utensils), the old Dominican convent a short way further along the road, and the Ethnographic Museum another 650m downhill.

As you leave Hermigua, a 4km return detour (to the right) would take you to the old port, where there's a natural rock pool dramatically set at the foot of a sheer escarpment — a tremendous setting. (*Note:* The best and safest swimming on the

Walkers ascending to the summit of La Fortaleza

island is on the south coast. The north is often rough and can be extremely dangerous: even the pool here is safe *only* when the sea is *dead calm!*)

Leaving this valley, you see Tenerife sitting across the water straight in front of you. A *mirador* (☎) allows you to pull over safely to admire it. Then, climbing high above the sea, you round a bend and look over what has to be the most beautifully-situated village on the island. **Agulo** (47km ♁ ⛰⛰⛰ ✕☎) is set in an alcove of rocky cliffs, high above the sea, looking straight out towards El Teide (*P*25a). Wander along the cobbled alleys that pass through the banana groves and admire the archetypal houses that give this village so much character. Walk 25 starts here.

The tunnel shown in the photograph on page 119 leads you out of Agulo's natural amphitheatre of cliffs into a deep, sheer-faced ravine. Rock walls rise above

you. Reaching the upper confines of this *barranco*, you come to **Las Rosas** (52km ✕), a scattered farming village. Fork left on a road signposted for La Palmita and the national park. Walkers and nature enthusiasts alike will find a wealth of information at the **Juego de Bolas**, the **Garajonay National Park Visitors' Centre** (*i*), 3km uphill. There's a typical Canarian dwelling, a display of local handicrafts, a film about the national park ... and even a bar/restaurant. Walk 25 — a strenuous hike — passes this way. However, Short walk 25-1 to the Mirador de Abrante with its awesome view over Agulo is only half the huff and puff — just a 55 minute round trip (see page 118).

Return to the junction in Las Rosas and turn left. After 0.3km you could take a 6.5km return detour to an out-of-the-way viewpoint and picnic spot — well worth the effort on fine

days. Turn up the steep bumpy lane that climbs to the square in Las Rosas. Continue straight up through the square to the Amalahuigue Reservoir. Cross the reservoir wall and then turn left, remaining on the same road all the way up. You climb a scruffy, shallow ravine as far as the tree line at Rosa de las Piedras. Visit the **Mirador Rosa de las Piedras** (☞✗*P*25b) on the crest of the ridge. From here, a vast cauldron stretches across in front of you, and ridges pour down into it. The restaurant Roque Blanco (closed Mondays) here serves up hearty local food in a friendly atmosphere.

The main tour, however, continues towards Vallehermoso. You look down into plunging ravines that drop off into the sea. Terraced vineyards ladder the slopes. These slopes produce the best wine on the island. Swinging inland, you wind around large open valleys,

passing above the pretty village of Tamagarda, noted for its typical oblong houses, all with tiled rooftops. Tamagarda's restaurant makes a mean *tortilla de ajo* (garlic omelette). Palms adorn the hillsides, and Roque El Cano, the massive lava pillar shown on page 122, bursts upon the scene: sitting like an exclamation mark, it punctuates the end of a trailing ridge.

Another tunnel takes you into the cauldron, and you're engulfed by hills. Roque El Cano looms overhead. The farming settlement of **Vallehermoso** (69km ✝▲✗🛒⊕) soon unfolds, tucked up against the valley walls. Dust-brown slopes climb back off it. A stream of banana plots, fruit trees and gardens flows down the valley floor, reviving the landscape. Walks 26 and 27 begin and end here.

Apart from the walking, whenever I reminisce about this village my thoughts turn to *miel de palma* — palm honey. It's made by boiling the palm sap and leaving it to cool into a dark syrup. Try this mouth-watering recipe: mix *gofio* (roasted maize flour; see the footnote on page 95) and the honey (as much as you like) into a doughy mixture, add pieces of white cheese (*queso blanco*), lemon rind, and ground almonds … and life will never be the same again! Sample the good local wine and the *mistela,* a local liqueur.

Turn right at the roundabout in the centre of Vallehermoso and, at the T-junction that follows, head right for the beach. *Please note* that the beach at **Playa de Vallehermoso** (71km ✗) is extremely dangerous at *all*

View from Los Roques, focusing on Roque de Ojila

times, hence the swimming pool nearby, which is only filled in summer. Some tourist books and brochures say that this is a good beach, but obviously no one has survived to tell otherwise! However, the setting, shown on page 126, is wonderful.

From the beach, return to the junction, and keep right to circle above Vallehermoso. Climbing out of the valley, its bucolic charm becomes more evident. You look out over adjoining valleys laced with palms. Plots of potatoes and tomatoes sit squeezed along the *barranco* floors and into the gentler pauses in the walls. The striking hamlet of Macayo captures your attention, its simple stone dwellings clinging to the side of a palm-studded ridge on your left. You can look down on this enchanting scene from the *miradores* a few bends higher up the road.

Approaching the summits, the countryside is scruffier, with scrub running down the declining ridges. In spring the route is splashed with resplendent yellow-flowering *codeso*. Near the tree-line you pass the Camino Forestal de la Meseta (82km *P26*; Walk 26) and then the turn-off for Alojera and Taguluche (83km). These isolated villages rest amongst dry, denuded hills, completely cut off by the cloud-catching *cumbre*. This scene will have much more impact from the Mirador Ermita del Santo later in the tour.

In the meantime, just around the bend, you come to the restaurant Chorros de Epina (✕). Just beyond it, turn right on a track branching off to the spring of **Chorros de Epina**, now a picnic site (🏕♦🖾). Stop here to

stretch your legs and admire the exquisite hamlet of Epina: follow the path behind the chapel for some minutes; in spring you'll stumble onto a habitat of the precious pink-flowering Canary geranium, and shortly thereafter you will be looking through the trees onto Epina, a neat little hamlet resting at the foot of the escarpment amidst green garden plots. Leaving Chorros de Epina, keep zigzagging uphill in the company of El Teide. Your vista sweeps back across the gently-declining coastal hills and over the numerous gullies segmenting the great cauldron. Heath trees, growing out of cracks in the rock, lean out over the road, and you disappear into the forest. At the Arure/Laguna Grande junction (the first you encounter), keep right. (A left turn would lead to two more picnic sites, located in a wonderful stretch of forest — Raso de la Bruma and Jardín de las Creces.) Approximately one kilometre further on you pass the *mirador* of **Alojera** (🖾).

Leaving the forest, descend to **Arure** (91km ✕; Walks 10-12), the home of a delicious honey. Some quaint stone cottages rest alongside the garden plots lining the floor of the *barranco*. At the end of the village (0.2km before the Valle Gran Rey junction), branch off right to the **Mirador Ermita del Santo** (🖾♦*P10*), unless you stopped there earlier in the day. This superb viewpoint hangs out from the escarpment high above Taguluche, a remote pocket of civilisation sitting deep in a bare landscape ruptured by upheavals of sharply-eroded hills. Heading home, follow your outgoing route back to **Valle Gran Rey** (102km).

☀ Walking

This book includes eight walks reached quite easily from a base in the **south of Tenerife**, but I've emphasised walking on **La Gomera**. (The companion volume, *Landscapes of Tenerife*, describes 60 long and short walks on that island — on the Teno and Anaga peninsulas, in the Orotava Valley, and around Las Cañadas.)

There are walks in this book for everyone.

Beginners: Don't be discouraged by the 'strenuous' grading given to many of the walks in the book. Start out by looking over the Picnicking section (pages 8-11): there you'll find five suggestions for Tenerife and 14 for La Gomera. Most of these make good, short and easy walks. On La Gomera you can also explore the signposted nature trails: a leaflet is available at the Centro de Visitantes Juego de Bolas at Garajonay National Park. Be sure to look, too, at the last paragraph on this page, about 'grading of the walks' on La Gomera.

Motorists: Walks suitable for those with cars (but not necessarily circular) are indicated by a ⊜ symbol in the Contents. *Almost* every walk can be done from a car — often it is one of the *variations* of the main walk that is recommended; look for the ⊜ symbol under 'Access'.

Experienced walkers: If you are used to rough terrain and have a head for heights, you should be able to tackle all the walks in this book — taking into account, of course, the season and weather conditions. For example, in rainy weather some of the walks will be unsuitable — especially the Barranco de Masca on Tenerife (Walk 8) and any walk on La Gomera involving narrow paths with steep ascents and descents. Always read the 'Grade' section of every walk you plan to do!

Regarding **grading of the walks**: Many of the walks on **La Gomera** have been written up with the bus time-tables in mind (although I have also included a number of circular walks for motorists). This means that several walks *ascend* inland and are thus graded as 'very strenuous'. These require good stamina and are only recommended for the hardy. Nevertheless, all these walks can be done in the reverse direction *(descending)*, simply by following the very detailed large-scale maps. Moreover, the longer walks can be cut in half. Thus most of the walks, in some permu-

35

tation, are accessible to everyone ... your only problems being transport and aching legs — if you tackle a walk with a very steep descent before getting used to the terrain.

Important: If you are not a reasonably fit walker, these walks may take you *much* longer than stated. *Do* take this into account when using public transport. I recommend that you start with a few of the shorter walks so you'll have some idea of how your pace compares with mine.

Caution is needed regarding terrain and weather. Some of the walks cross very remote country and can be both *very cold and potentially hazardous.* Distances on both islands can be very deceptive, with exhausting descents into and ascents out of hidden *barrancos* between you and your goal. Only link up walks by following roads, tracks or trails indicated on the walking maps. *Don't attempt to cross unmapped terrain; always be prepared for bad weather, and never walk alone.*

Guides, signposting and waymarking, maps

No **guide** is needed for any walk in this book, but should you wish to hire one to accompany you on a walk, ask at a tourist office or visitors' centre.

Signposting on both islands has been upgraded to European standards, but **waymarking** is minimal. Where it does exist, two types of route have been identified:

- long-distance footpaths ('Grandes Recorridos' or 'GR' routes), indicated by *red and white* waymarks;
- day trails of up to six hours ('Pequeños Recorridos' or 'PR' routes), indicated by *yellow and white* waymarks;

For both routes, horizontal stripes indicate 'continue this way', right-angled stripes show a 'change of direction'; an 'X' means 'wrong way'. Standard European waymarking also highlights local trails up to 10km long ('Senderos Locales' or 'SL' routes, marked *green and white*), but these do not feature on Tenerife or Gomera at present.

Most signs on **Tenerife** conform to the above guidelines, as can be seen in the photo on page 23, where PR trails are signed yellow/white. But in addition the Teide National Park has maintained its own longstanding system of route marking for 35 walks within the park. These are usually signed on metal plaques showing route numbers. On the map on pages 60-61 you can see three overlapping types of route: the long distance GR131, two different day (PR) walks and several national park trails. Tourist offices and visitors' centres all have maps showing local trails.

Gomera adopted the European standards in 2004, but has since abandoned the system of numbering and colour-coding PR routes (GR trails are still marked red/white).

Instead there are 40 signposted, government-maintained trails (see photograph on page 115), *plus* 18 marked trails in the Garajonay National Park. Since many *trail numbers are duplicated,* we have *not* shown them on our walking maps — it would be too confusing. But you can see all Gomera's trails on maps published by the island government (see www.lagomera.travel and search 'Hiking').

Important: the walks in this book *do not always follow the 'official' routes,* so please read the walking notes!

The **maps** in this book, originally drawn from 1:50,000 military maps, have been greatly adapted over the years as the walks are checked on the ground. Good government walking maps are usually available free at visitors' centres; some useful commercial walking maps have been published by Discovery, Freytag + Berndt and Goldstadt.

D ogs — and other nuisances

There are few nuisances to worry the walker on either Tenerife or La Gomera. The **dogs** tend to *look* more vicious than they really are — especially the shepherds' dogs. But your biggest concern is likely to be abandoned dogs trying to follow you back to wherever you are staying. Nevertheless, you may wish to invest in a 'Dog Dazer' — an ultrasonic device which persuades aggressive dogs to back off without harming them. These are available from various websites, including amazon.

Hunters blasting their shotguns will scare the wits out of you. I actually recommend not hiking on Thursdays, Sundays or public holidays during the autumn hunting season! Usually you hear hunters long before you see them.

You'll be happy to know that there are *no* poisonous snakes or insects on either island.

W eather

Island weather is often unpredictable, but there are a few signs and weather patterns that may help you forecast a walking day. Tenerife and La Gomera share much the same weather. Both are blessed with good walking weather all year round.

The north unfortunately has more than its fair share of rain, but boasts pleasant temperatures. The south soaks up the sun. Las Américas/Los Cristianos on Tenerife and Playa de Santiago on La Gomera enjoy the best weather. On La Gomera, Valle Gran Rey is slightly cooler and is prone to strong winds. Wind also strikes the southern coastline east of Los Cristianos, but rain is rare. During the winter months, the north not only suffers from clouds, but often experiences very strong winds, especially on the more open hilltops. Walking and keeping upright at the same time can be a problem!

Apart from the seasons, the **weather patterns** are influenced by two main **winds**: the *alisio*, the trade wind from the northeast, and the *tiempo del sur*, an easterly or southeasterly wind. The trade wind is identified by the low-flying fluffy clouds which hover over the north (between 600-1500m/2000-5000ft) for much of the year. On Tenerife, you can head to Las Cañadas to get above the clouds and enjoy clear blue skies. But on La Gomera, the *cumbre* (central mountain chain) and Garajonay usually remain deep in cloud — not much fun for walking, since it's cold and wet, with zero visibility. The walks in the north of La Gomera all disappear into cloud at some stage. Sometimes, however, the summits sit just above the sea of clouds, so that you have the wonderful sight shown in several of the photographs in this book.

The *tiempo del sur*, quite different, brings heat and dust. Temperatures rise considerably, and the atmosphere is filled with very fine dust particles. This weather is more frequent in winter than in summer. It seldom lasts more than three or four days. These days, outside of summer, are good for walking; even if it's a little warm, the sky is cloudless, although a bit hazy. (In summer it is *not* advisable to walk when the *tiempo del sur* is blowing; you risk sunstroke and dehydration, unless you are in a very shaded area.)

Two less frequent winds that could spoil your day are the nor'westerly from the North Atlantic and the sou'westerly from the tropics. Both bring heavy rains. This weather covers the entire island and can last a few days. When these winds blow in winter, Las Cañadas and El Teide are more likely to see snow than rain.

Remember (especially in winter) that no matter how wonderfully the day begins, it could deteriorate. **Always be prepared for the worst.** Along Gomera's *cumbre* the weather is less predictable still, and it can be *exceedingly cold*. Remember too, that the sun can be your enemy, perhaps especially on days of light cloud cover.

Where to stay

If you are based in Playa de las Américas or Los Cristianos in the **south of Tenerife**, the entire island is within reach if you have a hired car. A few superb walks are also nearby (Walks 1-8 in this book). The bus service is also excellent — you could even explore the Anaga Peninsula via Santa Cruz using the companion volume, *Landscapes of Tenerife*. Another advantage of staying at the *playas* is the proximity of the ferries — ideal for day trips to nearby La Gomera.

But if the sight of concrete jungles 'turns you off', try El Medano, Adeje, Granadilla, San Juan or Los Gigantes. For something really special, stay in a **rural hotel or house**: see www.ecoturismocanarias.com. Consider, too, spending a night at the Parador de las Cañadas before setting out on Walk 6 — a real treat! To book, log on to www.parador.es/en/parador-de-las-canadas-del-teide.

Exploring **La Gomera** from a base in southern Tenerife is the way many visitors will first become acquainted with this little-developed gem of an island. The car tours and some short walks are perfectly feasible on day trips.

But to get to know La Gomera on foot, you will want to be based on the island. Most visitors stay at Valle Gran Rey (try the Hotel Gran Rey, right on the beach, www.hotel granrey.es) or Playa de Santiago, followed by San Sebastián and, to a lesser extent, Hermigua and Agulo. San Sebastián's Parador (www.parador.es/en/parador-de-la-gomera, photograph on page 7) is set above the town, with great views. (Like the rest of the hotel, its good restaurant is themed around the era of Columbus, who set sail from San Sebastián on his first voyage across the Atlantic.) But there is also a good selection of self-catering accommodation, *pensions,* and rooms to rent all round the island. See the website for rural hotels and houses mentioned above, or surf the web.

Camping is forbidden anywhere inside the national parks.

What to take

If you buy this book on one of the islands, and you haven't brought any special equipment such as a rucksack or walking boots, you can still do some of the walks, or buy some equipment at one of the sports shops. Don't attempt the more difficult walks without the proper gear. For each walk in the book, the *minimum* equipment is listed. Where walking boots are required, there is, unfortunately, no substitute: you will need to rely on the grip and ankle support they provide, as well as their waterproof qualities. All other walks should be made with stout lace-up shoes with thick rubber soles, to grip on wet or slippery surfaces.

You may find the following checklist useful:

walking boots (which must be broken-in and comfortable)
waterproof rain gear (outside summer months)
long-sleeved shirt (sun protection)
first-aid kit, including bandages
walking stick(s)
windproof (zip opening)
map (see page 36)
spare bootlaces
sunhat, sunglasses, suncream

up-to-date bus timetable
small rucksack
plastic bottle with water-purifying tablets
long trousers, tight at the ankles
insect repellent
knives and openers
lightweight fleece, warm fleece
extra pair of socks
plastic groundsheet
torch, whistle, compass

Please bear in mind that I've not done *every* walk in this book under *all* weather conditions. Use good judgement to modify my lists according to the season.

Country code for walkers and motorists

The experienced rambler is used to following a 'country code' on his walks, but the tourist out for a lark may unwittingly cause damage, harm animals, and even endanger his own life. A code for behaviour is especially important on Tenerife and La Gomera, where the rugged terrain (and unexpected cold weather at high altitude) can lead to dangerous mistakes.

- **Only light fires** at picnic areas with fireplaces.
- **Do not frighten animals**. The goats and sheep you may encounter on your walks are not tame. By making loud noises or trying to touch or photograph them, you may cause them to run in fear and be hurt.
- **Walk quietly** through all hamlets and villages and take care not to provoke the dogs.
- **Leave all gates just as you found them**, whether they are at farms or on the mountainside. Although you may not see any animals, the gates *do* have a purpose: they keep animals in (or out of) an area. Again, animals could be endangered by careless behaviour.
- **Protect all wild and cultivated plants**. Don't try to pick wild flowers or uproot saplings. They will die before you even get back to your hotel. Obviously fruit and other crops are someone's private property and should not be touched. *Never walk over cultivated land.*
- **Take all your litter away with you.**
- **DO NOT TAKE RISKS!** This is the most important point of all. Do not attempt walks beyond your capacity, and do not wander off the paths described if there is any sign of mist or if it is late in the day. **Never walk alone**, and *always* tell a responsible person *exactly* where

you are going and what time you plan to return. Remember, if you become lost or injure yourself, it may be a long time before you are found. On any but a very short walk near villages, be sure to take a first-aid kit, torch, whistle, compass, extra water and warm clothing — as well as some high-energy food, like chocolate.

Spanish for walkers

In the tourist centres most people speak English. But once out in the countryside, a few words of Spanish will be helpful, especially if you lose your way. Here's a way to communicate in Spanish that is (almost) foolproof. First, memorise the few short key questions and their possible answers below. Then, when you have your 'mini-speech' memorised, always ask the many questions you can concoct from it **in such a way that you get a 'sí' (yes) or 'no' answer**. Never ask an open-ended question such as 'Where is the main road?' Instead, ask the question and then *suggest the most likely answer yourself*. For instance: 'Good day, sir. Please — where is the path to Epina? *Is it straight ahead?'* Now, unless you get a *'sí'* response, try: *'Is it to the left?'* If you go through the list of answers to your own question, you will eventually get a *'sí'* response — probably with a vigorous nod of the head — and this is more reassuring than relying solely on sign language.

Following are the two most likely situations in which you may have to practice some Spanish. The dots (...) show where you will fill in the name of your destination. Approximate pronunciation of place names is in the Index.

■ Asking the way

The key questions

English	Spanish	pronounced as
Good day, sir (madam, miss).	Buenos días señor (señora, señorita,	**Boo**-eh-nos **dee**-ahs sen-**yor** (sen-**yor**-ah sen-yor-**ee**-tah).
Please — where is	Por favor — dónde está	**Poor** fah-**voor** — **dohn**-day es-**tah**
the road to ... ?	la carretera a ...?	la cah-reh-**teh**-rah ah ...?
the footpath to ...?	la senda de ...?	lah **sen**-dah day ...?
the way to ...?	el camino a ...?	el cah-**mee**-noh ah ...?
the bus stop?	la parada?	lah par-**rah**-dah?
Many thanks.	Muchas gracias.	**Moo**-chas **gra**-thee-as.

Possible answers

English	Spanish	pronounced as
is it here?	está aquí?	es-**tah** ah-**kee**?
straight ahead?	todo recto?	**toh**-doh **rec**-toh?
behind?	detrás?	day-**tras**?

to the right?	a la derecha?	ah lah day-**reh**-chah?
to the left?	a la izquierda?	ah lah eeth-kee-**er**-dah?
above/below?	arriba/abajo?	ah-**ree**-bah/ah-**bah**-hoh?

■ Asking a taxi driver to return for you

English	Spanish	pronounced as
Please	Por favor	**Poor** fah-**voor**
take us to …	Ilévanos a …	Y**ay**-vah-nos ah …
and return	y volver	ee vol-**vair**
for us at …	para nosotros a …	**pah**-rah nos-**oh**-tros ah …

Point out the time when you wish him to return on your watch.

Walkers' checklist
The following points cannot be stressed too often:

- **At any time a walk may become unsafe** due to storm damage or road works. If the route is not as described in this book, and your way ahead is not secure, do not attempt to go on.

Cerrajón (Sonchus ortunoi)

- **Walks for experts only** may be unsuitable for winter, and all mountain walks may be hazardous then
- **Never walk alone.** Four is the best walking group: if someone is injured, two can go for help, and there will be no need for panic in an emergency.

Palo sangre (Sonchus tectifolius); below: *Taginaste rojo* (Echium wildpretii)

- **Do not overestimate your energies** — your speed will be determined by the slowest walker in your group.
- **Transport connections** at the end of a walk are vital.
- **Proper shoes or boots** are a necessity.
- **Mists** can suddenly appear on the higher elevations.
- **Warm clothing** is needed in the mountains; even in summer take some along, in case you are delayed.
- **Extra rations** must be taken on long walks.
  Compass, whistle, torch, first-aid kit weigh little, but might save your life.

- **Always take a sunhat with you**, and in summer a cover-up for your arms and legs as well.
- **A stout stick** is a help on rough terrain and to discourage the rare unfriendly dog.

Organisation of the walks

The walks in this book are located in the south and southwest of Tenerife and all over La Gomera. On La Gomera, the walks are arranged anti-clockwise around the island, starting from Valle Gran Rey (VGR). Bus journey times *from the nearest base* are indicated (eg, for Walk 11, plan on a journey of 35min from/back to Valle Gran Rey). This should make travel logistics easier.

You might begin by considering the large touring maps inside the back cover. Here you can see at a glance the overall terrain, main and secondary roads, and the locations of all the walks. Flipping through the book, you'll see that there is at least one photograph for every walk.

Having selected one or two potential excursions from the map and the photographs, turn to the relevant walk. At the top of the page you will find planning information: distance/time, grade, equipment, and how to get there. If the grade and equipment specifications are beyond your scope, don't despair! *There's almost always a short or alternative version of a walk,* and in most cases these are far less demanding of agility and equipment. If even these seem too tough, then turn to the Picnicking section on pages 8-11, for a good selection of easy walks.

When you are on your walk, you will find that the text begins with an introduction to the overall landscape and then quickly turns to a detailed description of the route itself. **Times** are given for reaching certain points in the walk. *Important: do* compare your own times with those in the book on one or two short walks, before you set off on a long hike. Remember that I've included only *minimal stops* at viewpoints; allow ample extra time for photography, picnicking, or swimming. The large-scale **maps** (all 1:50,000; see page 37) have been set out facing the walking notes if the route is isolated, but where several routes converge, they are presented on facing pages, to help with overall orientation. Below is a key to the symbols on the walking maps:

═══ expressway	●→ spring, tank, etc	♠/† church; shrine
─── main road	P picnic (pages 8-11)	⊢ cemetery
─── secondary road	PR TF 7 waymarked trail	🎋 picnic site with tables
─── track	👓 best views	
----- trail, path or steps	⁝ danger! vertigo!	⅄ pylon; mast
══6→ main walk	🚐 bus stop	⊞ map continuation
══12→ alternative walk	🚗 car parking	i visitor centre
─── watercourse, pipe	⚓ ferry port	☼ ∩ mill; cave
—400— altitude (metres)	■ specific building	◭ rock formation
	═══ park boundary	I I dyke; gate

Distance: 12km/7.4mi; 3h45min
Grade: moderate, with a stiff climb to the summit (428m/ 1403ft). One short stretch of path on the descent is narrow and exposed; you must be sure-footed and have a head for heights. *No shade en route.*
Equipment: walking boots, walking stick(s), sunhat, suncream, light fleece, raingear, picnic, plenty of water
Access: 🚌 (Timetables 2-4, 7-10) to/from Los Cristianos; alight at the Los Cristianos bus station on Avenida de Los Cristianos. Or ⛴ (Timetable 18) to the port. Or 🚗: park in Los Cristianos.
Short walk: Los Cristianos — Llano de Las Mesas — Los Cristianos (8km/5mi; 2h10min). Relatively easy ascent of 200m/ 656ft, *but no shade.* Equipment and access as above. Follow the main walk to the 50min-point, then turn right on the track and follow the notes from the 2h20min-point to the end.

Montaña Guaza is the oversized hill to the east of Los Cristianos. While it doesn't inspire you to put on your hiking boots straight away, it does make a most rewarding evening's hike, especially around sunset.

The walk starts from the **Avenida Marítima**, the seafront promenade (see plan of Los Cristianos on the fold-out map). Setting off from outside KING BURGER, just follow the promenade east all the way to the end, to the last hotel — the COSTAMAR. Turn left past the hotel and head through a parking area. Beyond the parking area, follow the track that passes behind the stony naturist beach.

Five minutes from the hotel (**15min**), take the hillside path by the SIGN 'MONUMENTO NATURAL MONTAÑA GUAZA'. Some 50m/yds uphill, make sure you swing left on the main, well-worn path; it will take you along a dry, dusty and stony hillside all the way to the top of the plateau. Prickly pear, candelabra spurge and *tabaiba* are the few inhabitants of this barren landscape. Ignore all descending paths.

Reaching the PLATEAU (**Llano de Las Mesas**), keep left along its edge, skirting above a valley. You briefly head alongside a watercourse (**40min**), before veering off right to cross abandoned terracing. Just after encountering the watercourse again, you come to the end of a track. Turn left here, still on a path, beside the valley.

You then meet another track (**50min**), where you turn left. *(But for the Short walk, descend this track to the right.)* As the ascent begins, fine views unravel. Montaña Rasca is the volcanic cone on the sea plain due south; the lighthouse of the same name stands behind it. Las Galletas is the first of the settlements. Further up the hillside, off a bend, you're overlooking a couple of pastoral outposts. In the winter, goatherds roam these hills. The track becomes rougher and steeper.

Forty minutes up the track, the way forks (**1h30min**). Keep right for the summit, a good five minutes uphill. The SUMMIT OF **Montaña Guaza** (428m/1403ft; **1h35min**) is decorated with various antennas. Your views stretch up the backbone of the island to the rim of Las Cañadas. Sharp pinnacles and ridges rise out of the barren landscape,

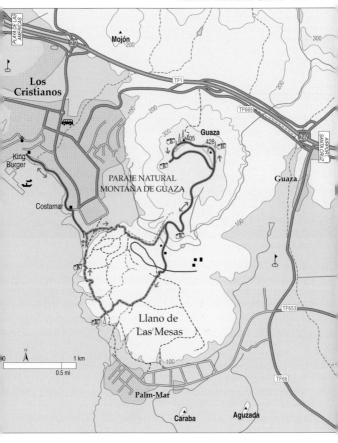

while bright white villages sprawl across the lower slopes.

From here a rough track takes you down to another summit (405m) with more aerials … and a bird's-eye view over Los Cristianos and Playa de las Américas further west. A couple of minutes more downhill, a two-minute detour to the right leads another viewpoint, directly above Los Cristianos. Circling the mountaintop, you rejoin your ASCENT TRACK (**2h05min**) and follow it downhill to the right. Ten minutes down, when you reach the bend in the track that lies above the pastoral outposts seen earlier, pause to trace out your onward route back to the coast. Looking a little further down the track, you'll see derelict buildings on either side of the track. Not far past these ruins, a clear path can be seen etched across the plateau immediately below, running towards the sea. That's your route, so keep it in mind.

Five minutes later you pass the point where you first joined the track on your ascent (**2h20min**). Continue straight ahead here for another seven minutes (or for

Paragliders enliven our descent back to the playas.

about four minutes below the derelict buildings). At this point the main track swings 90° left and a lesser track goes right. Keep straight ahead here, on a faint track, crossing another track forking off to the right. The track you are on quickly fades out, but your continuation, a faint path, can be seen up ahead — about 20° off to the right.

Less than ten minutes across the rock-strewn plain, a path joins from the left (**2h45min**): follow it to the right. Within the next five minutes, pass a turn-off left and come to a T-junction. Turn left here. At the next T-junction, two minutes later, go right. A large cone of gravel stands slightly to the left now — it's a good look-out point but, if you continue straight on past the cone to the clifftops, there's a good view over Palm-Mar, a small, desolate-looking tourist village to the left.

Now returning to Los Cristianos, keep left from the cliff-top viewpoint. In a couple of minutes a steep, slippery

descent takes you across a shallow *barranco*. Gaining the crest, Los Cristianos and Las Américas reappear. These resorts are seen at their best from the edge of the cliffs (**3h10min**), especially when the paragliders add their flourishes of colour to the landscape.

Follow the path along the cliff-tops until you come to a path forking off left. It will take you back down to the naturist beach. (A short stretch of path is vertiginous.) When the path frays out, all strands lead back down to the main outward path, where you swing left to reach the beach, some 20 minutes downhill. A further 15 minutes sees you back at KING BURGER (**3h45min**).

Walk 2: ROQUE DEL CONDE

Distance: 6.5km/4mi; 3h30min
Grade: a fairly strenuous ascent/descent of about 500m/1650ft overall. The final 100m/330ft of ascent to the summit of Conde is steep, stony and slippery (special care needed on the descent). The walk could be dangerous in wet weather or if the mountaintop is covered in cloud.
Equipment: walking boots,

walking stick(s), sunhat, suncream, warm fleece, windproof, raingear, picnic, water
Access: 🚐 to/from Arona (Timetables 4 and 6); journey time from Los Cristianos 20min. Or 🚗: park in Arona on the west side of the TF51 — or in Vento, near the start of the path proper, saving 25min overall.

The table-topped summit of Roque del Conde is the most prominent feature of the landscape in the south of Tenerife. Unlike Guaza (Walk 1), it *does* inspire you to put on the hiking boots — it's obviously a mountain that is there to be climbed. Its eye-catching shape also makes one feel that it was probably once a sacred mountain.

Candelabra spurge (Euphorbia canariensis) *and prickly pear cacti cover the lower slopes of Conde. Arona is the village in the middle distance.*

Alight from the bus at the last stop in **Arona** and **start the walk** by continuing straight ahead across the bridge over the TF51 (Los Cristianos/Vilaflor road). Then turn right immediately and head down to the road. Now follow the TF51 uphill for a few minutes, when you can turn left into the village of **Vento**, with its brown stone walls. Conde stands bold as brass straight before you here.

A little over five minutes along (**15min**), come to a junction with a STATUE OF CHRIST in the middle. Head left here and, after less than 100m/yds (just after house No 78), turn right on a lane. Then continue down the path that leads off it (there is a walkers' SIGNBOARD here). Passing between terraced gardens, after less than 50m/yds the path suddenly swings back to the right, dropping into the **Barranco de las Casas** below. Once on the far side, you pick up WHITE ARROWS waymarkers, which you'll follow for the rest of the hike.)

Out of the *barranco* you cross a crest, then dip into a side-*barranco* (**Barranco del Ancón**) full of rushes. In summer the countryside is as dry as a bone. The only plant life appears to be *tabaiba*, rock-roses and prickly pear. Just after stepping over a narrow WATER CHANNEL (**30min**), you descend a well-paved trail into the deep **Barranco del Rey**. Fig trees growing out of the valley walls supply the only greenery here. (Before climbing out of this *barranco*, head along to the left for a look at the high dry cascade.)

Out of the *barranco*, continue to the left. Paths head in all directions here, so follow the clear path and WHITE ARROWS — basically keeping left, beside the edge of the *barranco*. Rounding the hillside, you come to an ABANDONED BUILDING and plots (**50min**). From here you have a good view back down over Arona.

Your continuing trail lies behind the building. Minutes up, you pass above two WHEAT THRESHING FLOORS — the second is the larger and most impressive. The hillside above is

View north to the hills from Playa de Adeje: from left to right, Roque de los Brezos, Roque Imoque, and table-topped Roque del Conde

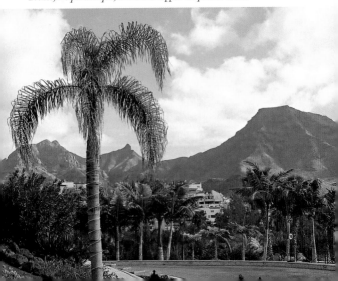

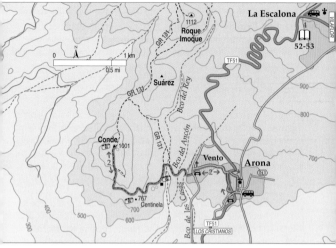

stepped with a mass of stone-walled terraces. Approaching the top of the crest, the previously well-manicured trail becomes a rough path. Large clumps of candalabra spurge and prickly pear abound, the latter covered in pale yellow blooms in late summer.

Mounting the **Centinela ridge** south of Conde (**1h15min**), you look down on the blinding-white swathe of the *playas* — Los Cristianos and Las Américas. Your immediate surroundings are severe and colourless. The path, unclear initially, continues to the right, around the slopes of Conde; keep an eye on the WHITE ARROWS AND CAIRNS. Several minutes along, a DYKE cuts across in front of you. Continue straight ahead; a steep winding ascent follows.

Less than 15 minutes above the dyke you meet a crossing contour path. Turn left along it and, 15 minutes later, you're at the SUMMIT OF **Conde** (**1h50min**). The first thing you'll notice is the remains of extensive terracing covering this tableland, testifying to intensive cultivation in the

past. The TRIG POINT is a rocky nodule a few minutes up to the left (1001m/3283ft). If you've beaten the clouds, you'll have a 360° view across the surrounding farm settlements, the coastal plain below, and the pine-speckled backbone of the island. To the right of the summit, you'll find another WHEAT-THRESHING CIRCLE, and to the left of that, a MEMORIAL PLAQUE. For the return, remember that the initial part of your descent is very steep and slippery! Around 10 minutes off the tableland, be sure not to miss your turn-off right from the contour path (where the tendency is to keep straight on).

Allow 1h30min to return to **Arona** (**3h30min**). When you reach the TF51, cross it and head into the back of the village. Keep right past the magnificent square, full of Indian laurel trees, to make for the BUS STOP at the end of the street. (Halfway along you'll pass the restaurant El Patio, where they serve up good, reasonably-priced cooking in a cool courtyard.)

Walk 3: ADEJE • BARRANCO DEL INFIERNO • ADEJE

See map overleaf
Distance: 8km/5mi; 2h55min
Grade: moderate climb/descent of 300m/1000ft. You must be sure-footed and agile. A few stretches of path are narrow and exposed. Do not attempt on windy or rainy days, as there is a danger of rock falls. The *barranco* may be impassable after heavy rain.
Important note: Because of its fragile ecosystem, this *barranco* is now within a Protected Natural Area; access is limited to 200 people per day, with no more than 80 people at one time. *You must book in advance to do this walk, choose your time slot for setting off, and arrive promptly.* The walk is open 08.30-17.30 daily *except public holidays*, and there is an entrance fee of 3 euros (Sundays free). It is best to book a day or so in advance. You can book in person or by telephone: 922 782 885 (English spoken). For more details see www.barrancodelinfierno.es.
Equipment: walking boots, sunhat, fleece, windproof, picnic, water
Access: 🚌 to/from Adeje (Timetables 5, 9); journey time from Los Cristianos 30min. *Travelling on Line 447*, alight at the 'Piedra Redonda' bus stop, and walk straight ahead north-east along Calle del Castillo to Calle de los Molinos and the start of the walk. *Travelling on Line 473*, alight at the 'Cerco' bus stop: walk uphill to the roundabout and then up Calle Grande, turning left by the church in the upper part of town to a large brown signpost for the *barranco*. Or 🚗: park in Adeje. If you arrive early enough, you can park in Calle Los Molinos, the street leading up to the *barranco* entrance. To get there, turn left by the church at the top end of Calle Grande (see map).

The Barranco del Infierno (Hell's Ravine) is probably the most walked gorge in the Canaries. So early in the morning is the quietest time for this ramble. This *barranco* boasts one of the few permanent streams on Tenerife. High sheer walls close in on you, as you make your way up the defile of jagged rock. Wild blackberry drapes itself over the trees and bushes, and ivy 'tunnels' convey you up to the splendid falls. Adeje is an immaculate village, with an appealing combination of old and new, set at the foot of the ragged crags that confine Hell's deep chasm.

The walk begins from CALLE LOS MOLINOS in the upper, older part of **Adeje**. If you come by car, turn left at the T-junction just beyond the CHURCH at the top of CALLE GRANDE (the tree-lined main street): follow signs directing you to the 'BARRANCO DEL INFIERNO'. If you come by bus Line 473, follow instructions for motorists; if you come by bus Line 447, walk up Calle del Castillo to Calle de los Molinos.

The path proper starts from the MIRADOR at the top of CALLE DE LOS MOLINOS. (You should *arrive well before* your allotted departure time to pay the entry fee and collect your ticket.) Take the path between the *mirador* and the Restaurante Otelo, descending to the right, into the *barranco*.
From the outset you're looking down into a dry ravine: further up the *barranco*, the water has

50

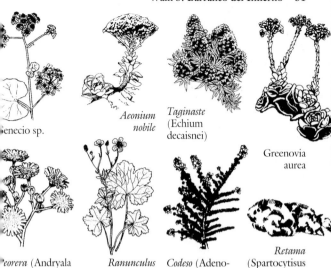

Senecio sp.

Aeonium
nobile

Taginaste
(Echium
decaisnei)

Greenovia
aurea

Feorera (Andryala
cheiranthifolia)

Ranunculus
cortusfolius

Codeso (Adeno-
carpus foliolosus)

Retama
(Spartocytisus
supranubius)

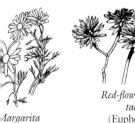

Margarita
(Argyranthemum)

Red-flowering
tabaiba
(Euphorbia
atropurpurea)

been diverted for irrigation into
watercourses and pipes. Clumps
of prickly pear, *balo* bushes and
tabaiba coat the steep slopes, and
white daisies grow alongside the
path. The route is obvious
throughout, so ignore all other
paths ascending the *barranco*
walls. Any potentially hazardous
edges are protected by wooden
fencing.

On rising to a *mirador,* **Acequía
Larga (30min)**, you enjoy a fine
view down the *barranco* and over
Adeje, built at the very edge of
the *barranco* walls. Fifteen
minutes later there is another
fine viewpoint. Soon after, you
descend to the floor of the
ravine.

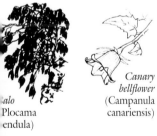

Balo
(Plocama
pendula)

Canary
bellflower
(Campanula
canariensis)

Vinagrera
(Rumex lunaria)

From here on the walk requires a
bit more agility, but this is the
most beautiful and most
dramatic part of the hike. When
you come upon the STREAM
(**1h**), the bed of the *barranco*
comes alive with willows and a
tangle of bramble, shrubs and
ferns. Pools become frequent
and, if you're early, you will see

Sea fennel
(Crithmum
latifolium)

The three-tiered waterfall cascades from a narrow dark defile, where the walls of the barranco *tower above you.*

and hear many birds. The rocky path criss-crosses the stream between the perpendicular walls of the gorge. Close to the end of the passable section of the ravine, a soft mossy rock face, dripping with water, is seen. It's a slithery couple of minutes' walk to the right to see the lovely WATERFALL shown left (**1h35min**). It splashes down some 80m/250ft into a small pool. The *barranco* walls tower 1000m/3300ft above you here, virtually blocking out the sky.

Allow about 1h20min to return to CALLE DE LOS MOLINOS for your car, and a few minutes more to walk on to your BUS STOP in **Adeje** (**3h**).

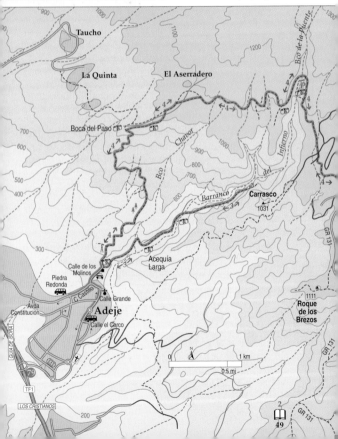

Walk 4: ADEJE • BOCA DEL PASO • IFONCHE • LA ESCALONA

Distance: 9.5km/5.9mi; 4h25min

Grade: strenuous, with an overall ascent of 850m/2790ft, 600m/1970ft of it continuous (the Alternative walk is an easier option). Most of the walk is waymarked with green/white flashes, indicating a *sendero local* (local walk).

Equipment: walking boots, walking stick(s), sunhat, warm fleece, windproof, picnic, plenty of water

Access: 🚌 to Adeje (Timetables 5, 9); journey time from Los Cristianos 30min. See notes on page 50 about bus stops in Adeje.

To return: 🚌 from La Escalona (Timetables 4, 7); journey time to Los Cristianos 25min

Short walk: Ifonche — Barranco del Infierno — Ifonche (5.5km/3.4mi; 1h30min). Moderate, with an overall ascent of 100m/330ft. Equipment as above. Access by 🚗: park near the highly-recommended and friendly Restaurante EL DORNAJO in Ifonche (closed Thursdays), 3.5km west of La Escalona, off the TF51. Facing the restaurant, take the road to the right of it. Just 50m/yds from the restaurant, turn right on a track. After another 50m you come to a faded signpost for Adeje. Turn off the track here, taking the trail that initially follows the line of a concrete WATER CHANNEL for 200m/yds. Keep to the main path — it is usually obvious on the ground and is well waymarked throughout with GREEN DOTS AND GREEN/WHITE FLASHES. Keep walking until you come to the floor of the **Barranco del Infierno**. It's worth carrying on and rising up the far side for 10 minutes or so — to where a spectacular view greets you as you look back across the *barranco* (**45min**). Return the same way.

Alternative walk: Escalona — Ifonche — Barranco del Infierno — Adeje (9.5km/5.9mi; 4h). Moderate, with ascents of about 200m/650ft and descents of 850m/2790ft overall. Equipment as main walk. Access: 🚌 to La Escalona (Timetables 4, 7); return on 🚌 from Adeje (Timetables 5, 9). See notes on page 50 about buses in Adeje. Walk along the ROAD from La Escalona to Ifonche (3.5km). Follow the **Short walk** above for **45min**, then use the map (and follow the waymarks) to continue down to **Adeje** (the main walk in reverse).

53

From the outset of this walk you'll huff and puff your way up to the cool and shady pine wood that sits unnoticed, 1000m/3300ft above sea level, sliding off the island's backbone. Views trail you all the way up. And if you've worked up an appetite, Restaurante El Dornajo, in the farming settlement of Ifonche, will serve you up a meal of such portions that you'll have to waddle down to the bus stop.

The walk begins in **Adeje**; see access details and follow Walk 3 on page 50. But where Walk 3 descends into the Barranco del Infierno, this walk ascends the small tarred lane to the left. A minute up, climb the path off to the right, signposted for IFONCHE (GREEN/WHITE SL WAYMARKS). The stony path zigzags up the rocky hillside, soon passing to the right of a RADIO MAST. The inclines are covered in the hardy omnipresent *balo, tabaiba,* and prickly pear. Five minutes up the path, you join another path: keep right. Your route will continue up this slope, eventually climbing to the top of the escarpment high above. Behind you lie the unexciting tourist developments splashed along the coastline.

Mounting a shelf set back in the hillside, you come upon remains of TERRACING (**45min**), with a few tired old almond trees. A few minutes later the way passes to the right of two pine trees. This makes an ideal rest stop. The path is unclear for about 100m/yds around here, but it continues in the same direction, then curves to the left; keep an eye open for the waymarks and be sure *not* to veer left off the main trail. A long arduous zigzagging ascent follows, and Adeje finally comes into sight.

The worst of the climbing is over when you reach the pass,

the **Boca del Paso** (**2h**). Now you can appreciate the panorama. Looking up the central massif, El Teide can be seen peering over the rim of the crater. Across the *barranco* to the left lie the farming villages of La Quinta and Taucho. To the right, pine woods stretch across the landscape.

Leaving the pass, swing right towards Ifonche immediately (ignoring the trail to Taucho). Either follow the water channel cut into the rock face, or take the path off right a few metres/yards further downhill; they will both emerge at the same place — below the few stone houses of El Aseradero which you can see over to the right, at the edge of the forest.

Minutes uphill from the pass you approach the cliff tops — and an excellent view over the surrounding countryside. The prominent flat-topped mountain to the south is Roque del Conde (Walk 2). In autumn, white-flowering asphodels fleck the top of this rocky ridge. Whether you followed the water channel or the lower path, the routes meet up to ascend the ridge climbing to the small derelict hamlet. Barely 20 minutes from the pass (**2h20min**), you come to a fork. The upper path continues up the ridge to within 200m of **El Aserradero**, then descends. Your route, the lower path, forks right to head round the hillside. In five minutes the upper path

Three hours into the walk the Barranco del Infierno tumbles away at your feet; Picnic 4 overlooks this barranco, *but from the other side.*

comes back down to join you.

Entering the trees, the way now winds in and out of small *barranco*s. Notice the absence of undergrowth here, typical of Canarian pine forests. Twenty minutes from the last fork (**2h40min**) you briefly enter a fairly large *barranco*. As you approach the crest of the ridge, ignore two faint forks (first to the right, then to the left). Some metres/yards beyond the second fork, follow the main trail sharply to the left, to pass over the crest. *Don't* take the path leading straight ahead (the right fork). Ten minutes further on, at a T-junction, turn left.

Soon (**3h**) the **Barranco del Infierno** tumbles away into a great chasm at your feet. Ifonche lies on the far side of it. Roque Imoque is the sharp, pointed peak in the background. The initial stretch of the descent into the *barranco* may prove unnerving for some walkers, although the trail is amply wide. Grand specimens of Canarian pine grow out of the valley wall. As you rise out of the *barranco*, ignore a path heading down to the right.

A good 10 minutes later you're out of the *barranco*. You cross a small gully and soon find a rock wall along the right-hand side of the trail. Ignore the fork ascending to the left just where you encounter this rock wall for the first time; your way is down to the right, and you cross a track in the valley floor 10 minutes beyond the Barranco del Infierno. Ignore another track going off to the right almost immediately. Continuing on the path out of this gentle valley, you cross another track and climb to the left of an amphitheatre of terracing.

Crossing the last crest you'll see **Ifonche**'s restaurant El Dornajo not far ahead. Meeting a track at a signpost, follow it downhill. Keep left to EL DORNAJO (**3h45min**; closed Thursdays). Leaving the restaurant, head left on the tarred road to La Escalona, 3.5km downhill (about 40 minutes' walk). The BUS STOP in **La Escalona** is 50m/yds up the TF51, to the left (**4h25min**). *Another option, if you don't like road-walking, is to follow the well signposted and waymarked GR131 from Ifonche to Arona (allow 1h30min).*

Walk 5: BOCA TAUCE • MONTAÑA DEL CEDRO • BOCA TAUCE

Distance: 9.75km/6mi; 3h
Grade: relatively easy, with 210m/700ft of ascent. Broom bushes crowd some of the paths. A short stretch of path requires a head for heights.
Equipment: hiking boots, long trousers, sunhat, warm fleece, windproof, gloves, raingear, picnic, plenty of water
Access: 🚐 to/from the 'Boca Tauce' bus stop (Timetable 4); journey 1h from Los Cristianos.

Or 🚘: park at Boca Tauce, by the national park information booth (Car tours 1 and 2).
Short walk: Boca Tauce — Roques del Cedro — Boca Tauce (7.8km/4.8mi; 1h40min). Easy; equipment and access/return as above. Follow the main walk to the turn-off for Montaña del Cedro (1h-point). Here keep straight on to the **TF38**, passing the **Roques del Cedro**. Return the same way.

Here's an easy walk for everyone. If you're just out for a stroll, do the Short walk. But the main walk is well worth the time invested: in three hours you'll cross a lava field and a *cañada* (a sunken plain of gravel), climb to a pass with superb views over the southern corner of Las Cañadas, and briefly head through a pine wood.

Begin the walk at the **Boca Tauce** JUNCTION: walk west along the TF21 to a small stone building (*CASA DE OFICIOS BOCA TAUCE*; **5min**). Then take the footpath just inside the chained entrance here. The path descends to the right amidst broom bushes 2m/6ft high, towards the lava field below. Hemmed in between the undulating crater wall on the left and the sea of jagged lava on the right, the way is straightforward. Small piles of stones help keep you on course, and green metal plates indicating 'SENDERO 18' mark the way.

Soon you encounter pines growing out of the crater walls. Sharp pinnacles of rock rise above you. On this side of the crater, the volcanic cone of Pico Viejo commands your attention, while El Teide stands in the background. At times you'll need to barge your way through the broom.

Soon (**10min**) you'll be crossing a corner of the lava flow. It's an intriguing sight (Picnic 5), but very jagged underfoot. Some minutes off this scoriaceous lava, you pass to the right of a second type of lava, known as *pahoehoe* ('ropey') lava, which resembles coils of rope.

Montaña del Cedro is now not far ahead. You cross a *cañada* and then pass by the foot of a large rock covered in orange and green lichen (**Chavao; 45min**). It gives a brief shady respite from the sun, but if you stop to rest here, note that there's a lot of broken glass about.

Just past this rock, you'll see a track above you, descending the crater wall. On your return you will be re-entering the crater through this pass. Keep to the right here, alongside the wall of the crater; a faint track comes underfoot; it soon becomes well defined.

Five minutes from the lichen-covered rock, step over a wire rope (that prevents vehicle access), and join the track descending from the pass.

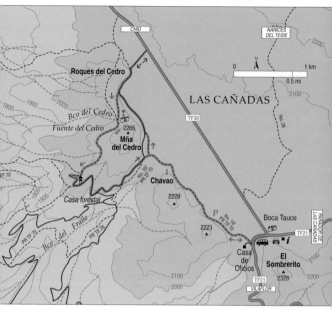

Follow it to the right. Less than 10 minutes along (**1h**), at a point where the track curves to the right, leave it: turn left, to begin the ascent of Montaña del Cedro (BOULDER, YELLOW DOTS). *(Those doing the Short walk should, however, remain on the track. Five minutes further on you will pass near the Roques del Cedro and then reach the TF38.)*

Beginning the ascent, you will have to push your way through bushes of broom. Small CAIRNS guide you. The path very quickly bears left to ascend the escarpment, and then becomes clear. A very short stretch of path along here may prove unnerving for those who have no head for heights.

Crossing a PASS (**1h15min**), you have a stupendous view through pine trees over onto Pico Viejo and its surrounding apron of lava. El Sombrerito is the peak that rises to the right of Boca Tauce, and further along the wall

is flat-topped Montaña Guajara (Walk 6).

Rounding the flanks of **Montaña del Cedro**, the southwestern corner of the island opens up, and a large ravine (**Barranco del Cedro**) slips away below you. On clear days you can see La Gomera and the veins of its ridges. El Hierro lies on the horizon behind it. And the two humps that usually float above the clouds are La Palma.

A couple of minutes above the pass, the path forks. Bear right below a broom bush and continue to climb, with YELLOW DOTS on rocks marking the way. A minute later you clamber over rocks to reach a SPRING IN A CAVE, the **Fuente del Cedro**. A tiny SHRINE sits in the rock face above it.

Higher up, you trail through a light pine wood. Rounding the hillside, a bright-red fire-watch tower comes into sight not far

Above: crossing a pass (1h15min), there is a fine view over to the flat-topped summit of Montaña Guajara.
Left, top: Pico Viejo, from above the Roques del Cedro (Short walk); bottom: crossing the lava flow, ten minutes into the walk (Picnic 5)

below. Shortly after spotting the tower, the path swings along the ridge towards it. The route is indistinct at times, but small PILES OF STONES show you the way. Soon you're standing below the FIRE-WATCH TOWER (**1h40min**). When they are stationed here, the forestry guards love to have a chat. If you're lucky (and although it's probably against regulations), they'll probably take you up top to see the fine view.

Heading on, follow the forestry track and, at the junction 10 minutes along, ascend to the left. Around 15 minutes uphill you re-enter **Las Cañadas** (**2h05min**). From the rim of the crater, follow the path down to the lichen-covered rock (**Chavao**) first encountered at the 45min-point.

From here on follow your outgoing path back to Boca Tauce, keeping an eye on the CAIRNS. Catch your bus at the **Boca Tauce** JUNCTION (**3h**), opposite the information booth.

Walk 6: PARADOR DE LAS CAÑADAS • PAISAJE LUNAR • VILAFLOR

Distance: 21km/13mi; 6h35min. You can shorten the walk by 3.5km/2.2mi; 40min if you take an early morning taxi to the start and catch the afternoon 🚌 342 from Lomo Blanco (Timetable 4).

Grade: strenuous and long, with an ascent of 210m/690ft and descent of 800m/2625ft. Recommended for experienced walkers: the descent into the Paisaje Lunar is very steep and slippery, and the waymarking is sometimes hard to follow.

Equipment: walking boots, walking stick(s), sunhat, fleece, gloves, windproof, raingear, picnic, plenty of water

Access: 🚌 to the Parador de las Cañadas (Timetable 4); journey from Los Cristianos 1h15min

To return: 🚌 from Vilaflor (Timetables 4, 7); journey time to Los Cristianos 35min

Shorter walk: Parador — Degollada de Guajara — Parador (8.5km/5.3mi; 2h40min). Moderate climb and descent of under 250m/820ft; equipment/access as main walk (or 🚗). Follow the main walk to the **Degollada de Guajara** (1h 30min); return the same way.

Alternative walk: Use the map to walk the **PR TF 72** circuit from Vilaflor to the Paisaje Lunar that also takes in part of the **GR 131**. It is highlighted in purple on our map (showing surfaces underfoot: tar, track, path); allow 2h30min out, 2h back. *This could be an excellent alternative*

Constantly-changing landscapes are encountered on this long hike: the stark splendour of Las Cañadas; the sprawling black-sand slopes of Montaña de las Arenas; the sandstone moulds of the Paisaje Lunar; and the forest of old Canarian pines. The real Canarian pine is the noble among peasants, and the pines of Vilaflor are renowned for their grandeur. Paisaje Lunar (the 'Moon Landscape') is the focal point of the walk: soft creams, beiges, yellows, browns and greys saturate its smooth conical formations.

Start out at the **Parador de las Cañadas**. Follow NATIONAL PARK TRAIL NO. 4 from the turning circle by the building. Your destination is the prominent mountain protruding out of the crater wall southeast of the Parador. In under 15 minutes the trail takes you to a tarred lane. Straight across is National Park Trail No. 31; ignore it and turn left to continue east along Trail No. 4. A fascinating formation of pink and yellow rocks rises just in front of you. The pastel colours give this fine natural sculpture its name — **Piedras Amarillas** ('Yellow

Stones'; Picnic 6). Behind them, you cross a small *cañada* (gravel plain), the **Cañada del Capricho**. Another *cañada* follows. Here **Guajara** — the bastion of the encircling walls — is seen at its best, rising 500m/ 1640ft from the crater floor. Splashes of yellow lichen, like paint daubs, decorate the higher rock faces. In spring, *taginaste rojo* — which may grow to 3m/10ft — adds bold strokes of red to this canvas.

Your ascent begins at the **50min-mark**, five minutes beyond a turn-off to the left (National Park Trail No. 15).

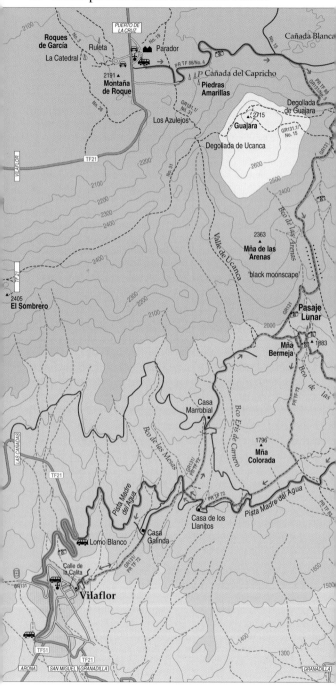

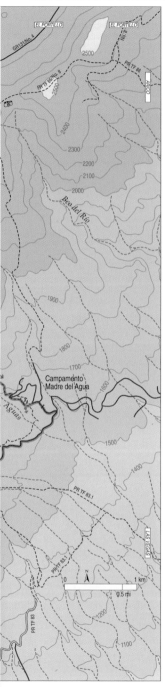

Here you join the **GR 131** (and
other trails) to begin the ascent.
Turn right uphill (red/white/
yellow waymarks). You reach
the edge of the crater at a pass,
the **Degollada de Guajara**
(2373m/7785ft; **1h30min**).
The views are magnificent. The
tones of the landscape flow into
and across each other. *(The
Shorter walk returns from here.)*
Crossing the pass, ignore paths
right (to Guajara's summit) and
left (National Park Trail No. 8
to El Portillo and PR TF 86 to
Villa Arico). Soon Gran Canaria
is in view: it seems surprisingly
close from this vantage point.
After a brief ascent, the path
forks (by a METAL POLE; **1h
40min**). The right fork is the
main ascent route to Guajara;
keep left for Paisaje Lunar.
Barely a minute down from the
turn-off, the path forks again:
keep right with the **GR 131**. Over
to your right (still in the
distance) is **Montaña de las
Arenas**, with its charred sides
and maroon summit. At the foot
of this sandhill lies a patch of
black sand, encircled by pines.
Your route descends straight
down through the middle of this
patch of black sand. Below you,
pines full of character dot the
landscape.
The path turns down a low side-
ridge. You pass a large PINE TREE
(**2h15min**) — a cool resting
place. Minutes below it, you're
trudging across the gravelly
black sand. Rocks flank your
route all the way downhill.
Ignore all turn-offs; keep
straight down.
Just before the end of the
sandhill and the first pines, the
trail forks. Ignore the path
straight ahead down the hill; go
right here, towards a large pine.
Beyond the pine, scramble down
a steep, gravelly bank —

probably on all fours. You cross the **Barranco de las Arenas** (where you could make a short detour back up the riverbed to a 'black moonscape').

From the floor of this ravine you ascend a gravelly ridge at the edge of another, lower ravine — the **Barranco de las Aguas**, home of the Paisaje Lunar. From this path you enjoy a first view down into the 'moon landscape'. When you come to a crossing trail, turn left downhill on the white/yellow waymarked **PR TF 72**. Follow this to a viewpoint

with a WALKERS' SIGNBOARD (**3h15min**).

Now *leave* the PR trail and head back the way you came. *(But for the Alternative walk continue on the PR TF 72.)* You come to a junction where the Paisaje Lunar is signed down to the right.

Descending carefully, you're soon walking along the very edge of the **Paisaje Lunar**. At another path junction, head right, alongside the *barranco*. Crossing a crest, you encounter a WATER PIPE, and minutes later you rejoin the left fork, heading right. When you meet a track, follow it to the right: a minute downhill, a picturesque campsite comes into view through the pines. Cut down through the camp, keeping straight downhill, and in a couple of minutes you'll reach the front entrance to **Campamento Madre del Agua** (**3h45min**). There's a water tap just above the office, to the right of the gate, should you need refuelling; *remember that you have 10km more to go!*

Turn right at the junction 400m/yds below Madre del Agua and follow this wide gravel track (taking in a couple of **PR TF 72** shortcut trails) for two hours — all the way to **Lomo Blanco** (**5h55min**), where it meets the TF21. You can catch the El Portillo bus here if you made an early morning start. Flag the bus down 100m/yds up to the right. If you're descending to **Vilaflor**, allow another 40 minutes along the main road (**6h35min**).

At the 2h15min-point a large pine provides welcome shade on a hot day (above left); beyond this point rocks flank your route all the way downhill (above right, taken just below the large pine, looking back up the descent path). Left: Some years ago it was possible to descend into the Paisaje Lunar, where smooth eroded fingers of pumice in soft pastel tones grow out of the ravine walls. This is no longer allowed — the area is under protection. But strangely enough, once I was down amongst them, these funnels looked somewhat less impressive than they did from above.

Distance: 6.5km/4mi; 2h40min
Grade: moderate, with ascents/descents of some 400m/1300ft overall (almost continual ups and downs), on very rocky terrain. You must be sure-footed and have a head for heights, and don't attempt in wet or windy weather. Orange waymarks; some cairns
Equipment: walking boots, sunhat, fleece, raingear, windproof, picnic, plenty of water
Access: 🚌 (Timetable 8) at 09.35 to Santiago del Teide, to connect with 🚌 355 from Santiago to Araza (Masca bus, not in the timetables; *recheck all times in advance*): departs at 10.35; returns 16:25, 18.25; journey time 10min. Or 🚗: Araza lies on the only track branching west off the TF436 between Santiago del Teide and Masca; park in the lay-by for the Mirador de Masca, about 200m above the turn-off (the third parking area you come to, approaching from Santiago).
Alternative walk: Araza — Finca de Guergues — Araza

(10km/6.2mi; 4h). Grade, equipment and access as main walk, but this hike is fairly strenuous, with ascents/descents of some 550m/1800ft overall, and the path is more slippery (take walking sticks if you use them). Follow the main walk to **La Cabezada** (**1h25min**), then descend the path to the left of the threshing circle. Pass a water tank built into the hillside a minute downhill; immediately beyond it, the path veers off to the right. *Pay close attention to the cairns from here on.* About 15 minutes down you reach **Los Pajares**, a lone house on a jutting rock. Your route swings to the right above the building, and descends to the right of another threshing floor. Remain on the right-hand side of the steep valley wall. Just above **Finca de Guergues**, you'll see another water tank on your left. Ignore the fork-off left immediately beyond it (and remember this fork for your return). You should reach the hamlet in **1h55min**; allow 2h05min to return to **Araza**.

H ere's an opportunity to taste the pleasures of the Masca Valley, without the slog — or hazards — of Walk 8! This hike offers spectacular views as you wind along a high jagged neck of land. *Barrancos* fall away on either side, hundreds of metres below. On the left lies the Barranco Seco del Natero, its slopes carpeted in shades of green; on the right the Barranco de Masca is concealed below precipitous walls.

Start out at the track to the farmstead of **Araza**, where there is usually a 'NO TRESPASSING' SIGN. Take the footpath just to the right of the track, marked by small CAIRNS. When it forks after 60m/yds, head uphill to the right — to a viewpoint with a plunging view over the Masca Valley (Picnic 7). Then return to

the fork and continue descending the crest of the ridge. Six minutes downhill, on a SADDLE, boulders block off a path on the left descending from the farm; ignore the path off left here into the Natero *barranco*.
Crossing bedrock — rich red, rose, maroon and brown — the way is at times vague, but stone-

laid sections of old trail keep re-appearing (watch, too, for the CAIRNS). Yellow-flowering broom and glossy green-leafed *tabaiba* brighten the hillsides. After passing through a GATE, you are soon enjoying continuous views down into *both* ravines, as you stride along the backbone of the ridge. Clinging to the slope, the path dips across a narrow neck of rock. Slowly, the southern coastline unravels: Los Gigantes, Playa de las Américas, and Los Cristianos are impressive sights. Table-topped Roque del Conde (Walk 2) sits on the far horizon inland from Los Cristianos.

Not long before the highest point, the trail moves briefly to the right-hand side of the ridge, and the terrain drops away abruptly; some people might find this short (10m/yds) stretch of path unnerving. The views over the **Barranco de Masca** are superb. But the sheer-sided peak ahead blocks out everything else for the moment, leaving you wondering: what lies beyond it? Reaching the HIGHEST POINT OF THE TRAIL (1034m/3400ft; wooden post), the least expected sight appears: green terraced slopes, stepped with rocks. A couple of stone huts nestle on the hillside not far below to your right. It's an exhilarating sight.

In just a few minutes you're at the houses at the top end of the high meadow, **La Cabezada**

View east over the Barranco Seco del Natero, from the threshing floor at Los Pajares.

(**1h25min**). A large circular stone-laid floor, once used for threshing the wheat and barley that was grown here, sits above the dwellings. Its simple design makes it very impressive. This setting, high on the edge of a rocky ridge, commands breathtaking views of the rest of this upheaval of basalt. But for the twitter of a few birds and the distant bleating of goats, the valleys are deathly quiet. La Gomera is clearly visible directly to the south. The tiny hamlet below, precariously perched at the edge of the Barranco Seco del Natero, is the Finca de Guergues (Alternative walk). Returning to Araza, your views stretch all the way back to El Teide. Be sure to flag your bus down *above* the **Araza** track, and well off the corner (**2h40min**).

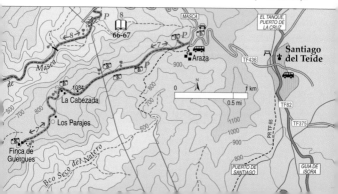

Walk 8: MASCA • BARRANCO DE MASCA • PLAYA DE MASCA • MASCA

See also photo on page 13
Distance: 9km/5.6mi; 6h
Grade: very strenuous, potentially hazardous descent/ascent of 600m/1950ft; recommended for very experienced hikers. You must be sure-footed and have a head for heights. *Do not attempt in wet or windy weather.*
Equipment: walking boots, walking stick(s), sunhat, raingear, fleece, windproof, whistle, plenty of water, picnic
Access: 🚐 to Playa de San Juan/Los Gigantes (Timetable 9); journey time from Los Cristianos 55min, then taxi to Masca (arrange for the taxi to collect you for your return bus). Note that 🚐 355 to Masca from Santiago del Teide doesn't allow enough time to finish the walk.) Or 🚗: park in Masca (the 'official' car parking areas fill up quickly; *arrive early!*).

Shorter walk: Masca — weir — Masca (2.5km/1.6mi; 2h15min). Strenuous descent/ascent of 200m/650ft. Equipment as above; access as Walk 7, page 64. Follow the main walk to the WEIR; return the same way.
Alternative walk: Masca — Playa de Masca (4.5km/2.8mi; 2h45min). Equipment and grade as main walk (you must be sure-footed and agile, but this avoids the return ascent). Access: 🚐 and taxi as above or 🚐 from Santiago to Masca (as Walk 7, page 64). Return: Pre-arrange for a Masca—Los Gigantes cruise ⛴ to collect you at the beach (tel: 922 861918). *These boats only run when the sea is calm! Double-check* days and times of sailings (usually at 13.30, 15.30, 16.30), *and make sure you have a voucher or ticket.* Follow the main walk to the beach.

The Barranco de Masca lies hidden in the huge block of roughly-dissected basalt that covers the north-western corner of the island. One of Tenerife's most popular trails, this walk drops you from the village of Masca (600m/1950ft) to the sea. Sheer jagged walls — in places just a few metres apart — rise above a boulder-strewn floor, leaving only just enough space to squeeze through.

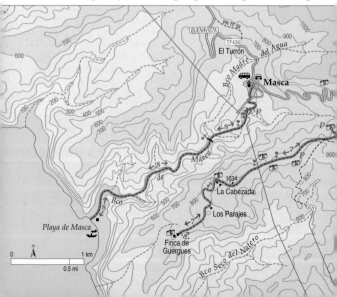

Walk into the village of **Masca** on the stone-paved lane that passes to the left of the CHURCH, where **the walk begins**. Just below the square, turn right on a paved path. A beautiful descent follows, with bougainvillea of all colours billowing out over the walls. The village has been prettily manicured, with stone walls, stone-laid paths and stone houses. A couple of minutes down, you're in a lower part of the village, on the ridge between the Barranco de Masca on the left and the Barranco Madre del Agua to the right. Here the lane you first followed curves in front of you again: follow it to the right. Some 40m/yds along, a signpost alerts you to your trail down left into the **Barranco de Masca**. A steep and very slippery descent follows.

The *barranco* is a contrast of dramatic rock forms and verdant scenery; at the outset, the slopes are littered with palms. Reaching a dyke in the valley wall, the path forks: you can go either side of the dyke. Ahead, the *barranco* walls rise perpendicularly. At a SIGN ('ESPACIO NATURAL PROTEJIDO'; **10min**) the way veers off to the left. When you

In the Barranco de Masca

In Masca

come face to face with an enormous boulder, circle to the left of it. A very steep, vertiginous descent follows, and you soon cross a WOODEN BRIDGE (**25min**; Picnic 8). The way heads left uphill from the bridge for a few metres, but then curves right, rounding a sheer escarpment — this vertiginous spot requires negotiation on all fours. The *barranco* floor is choked with cane ... not that you'll care to notice at this point. You'll probably be surprised to find terracing even on these precipitous walls.

Three more barranco crossings bring you to a LOW WEIR, where the **Barranco Madre del Agua** comes in from the right (**55min**). The Shorter walk turns back here but, first, some exploring. *Carefully* scramble up the slippery rock on the right, into the Barranco Madre del Agua. Hidden in amongst the rock and cane lies a deliciously cool, thigh-deep pool.

At the confluence, the Barranco de Masca becomes a narrow shaded chasm and veers left, heading for the sea. A narrow *canal* (watercourse) is built into the left-hand wall of the gorge. Descend the flood control wall on the left. Cross the river bed

and, from here on, you can't possibly lose your way (it is even CAIRNED).

To reach the beach from here takes about another 90 minutes' clambering over rocks and boulders, occasional ankle-deep wading (depending on rainfall, irrigation requirements, and the season) and climbing up old, crumbled paths. The indented craggy walls rise precipitously above you — in some places as high as 700m/2300ft. Several small pools add to the cool freshness of the *barranco*.

Eventually you're on a stony beach, the **Playa de Masca** (**2h30min**), more than likely looking out onto a flotilla of tourist cruise boats anchored off the shore. The building here (a private house) is by no means an eyesore; its stone construction blends in with the landscape, and the enclosure full of various trees enlivens the mouth of the valley. Depending on the tide, there may be a sandy beach over to the left. But the small jetty built into a large rock over to the right makes an ideal spot for swimming and picnicking. Refresh yourself for the uphill slog. Allow yourself an *extra* hour for the return the **Masca** (**6h**).

68

Walk 9: BARRANCO DE ARURE

Distance: 3.25km/2mi; 2h
Grade: fairly easy, with an ascent of just under 200m/650ft. You must be sure-footed and agile: most of the hike is up the *barranco* bed, clambering over and around rocks. Avoid after heavy rain. Waymarked with arrows, dots and some wiggly designs indicating water.
Equipment: walking boots, sunhat, fleece, picnic, water
Access: 🚌 or 🚐 (Timetables 11, 16) to/from Casa de la Seda; journey time from Valle Gran Rey 10min. Park in the long roadside car park between El Guro and Casa de la Seda.

The Barranco de Arure, an idyllic offshoot of the Barranco Valle Gran Rey, is the equivalent of Tenerife's Barranco del Infierno. Both lie in deep rocky ravines, and both boast a decent-sized (for the Canaries, anyway) waterfall. This walk is one big, fun Indiana Jones agility test: scramble over rocks, boulders and fallen tree trunks, creep through dense vegetation and pull yourself up on lianas and branches. Great fun for young and old, but you must be agile!

The hike starts at the northern (**Casa de la Seda**) end of the long roadside CAR PARK, where the bus also stops. Walk north up the road towards Los Granados. Just as the road kinks to the right (and immediately after a garage with some vines on top) take the concrete and stone path ascending to the left, signposted 'CAMINO BARRANCO LOS ANCONES'. Behind the first house, your route suddenly swings right up the rocky hill-face; arrows and dots on a stone wall indicate the turn-off. You circle above the valley floor, which is full of fruit trees and garden plots. Three minutes from the road, at a faint fork, keep left on the lower path. Severe, dark jagged basalt walls rise above you, a sharp contrast to the verdant valley floor.

Soon you enter the bed of the **Barranco de Arure** (**5min**; Picnic 9) and follow it to the right. From here the route lies mainly in the stream bed. A number of other paths criss-cross the valley floor.

Clumps of papyrus grass grow along the stream bed, which contains only a trickle of water at

Waterfall in the Barranco de Arure

69

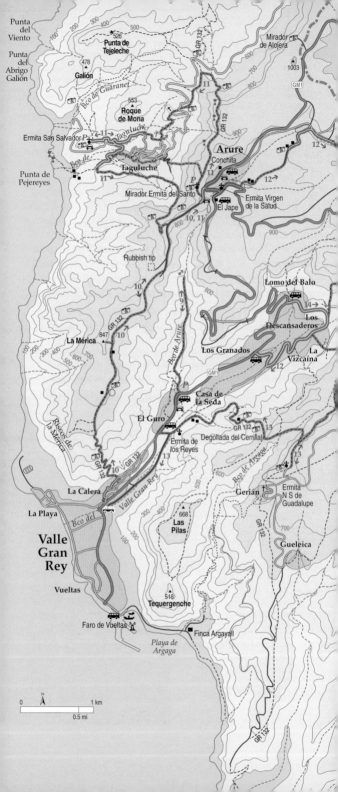

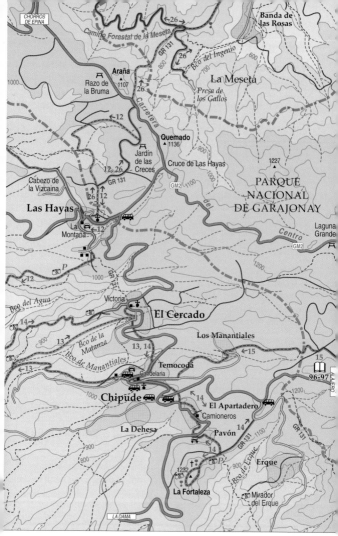

this stage. At times the way is
through a corridor of Indian
cane. Higher up, stringy willows
begin to appear.

As the course of the riverbed
changes every year after heavy
rainfall, and the amount of water
it carries varies with the seasons,
your path may change from year
to year. There may be side paths
up the banks at times to avoid
difficult passages, or there may
be small scrambles next to
miniature waterfalls, sometimes
with the help of a rope. But for
most of the time the way follows
the *barranco* bed. *Always make
sure of your footing on wet surfaces!*
The higher up you get, the
more water the stream carries
and eventually the sound of
gurgling water is all around you
until, finally, you reach the foot
of a 15m/50ft-high *WATERFALL*
in a cool dark rock cauldron
(**1h**).

Allow an hour for the return to
Casa de la Seda (**2h**). Catch the
bus back to Valle Gran Rey from
the *BUS STOP* here.

Walk 10: FROM VALLE GRAN REY TO ARURE

See map pages 70-71
Distance: 8km/5mi; 3h15min
Grade: very strenuous, with an overall ascent of 800m/2600ft. Red and white waymarking (GR 132). *Note:* The walk can easily be done as a descent from Arure, taking 2h15min. Access by 🚐 as for the Shorter walk; see map on pages 70-71.
Equipment: walking boots, fleece, windproof, sunhat, raingear, picnic, plenty of water
Access: on foot; 🚐 to La Calera (Timetables 11, 16); or ⛴ to Vueltas (Timetable 18), then on foot to La Calera
To return: 🚐 from Arure (Timetables 11, 16); journey time to Valle Gran Rey 35min.
Shorter walk: La Mérica from

Arure (7km/4.3mi; 2h25min). Easy ascent/descent of 100m/330ft; equipment as above. Access: 🚐 or 🚐 (Timetables 11, 16) to Arure. The walk proper starts on the lane to the **Mirador Ermita del Santo**, which turns west off a hairpin bend in the main road. By car, park opposite Bar Conchita in the centre and walk 500m/yds downhill to the turn-off on your right. By bus, alight at the Bar/Restaurant El Jape and walk north along the road, past the Las Hayas turn-off, to the first turning left. This tarmac lane reverts to track after 200m/yds. Use the map on pages 70-71 to reach the triangulation point on the **La Mérica** summit and return the same way.

This walk scales the precipitous rock walls that overshadow La Calera and then heads north. The really fit will start out from Valle Gran Rey early in the morning and watch the sun creep slowly over the *barranco* below. Those who prefer a more leisurely approach can descend the well-graded route from Arure. Climbing or descending, your views dip into every nook and cranny of the Gran Rey ravine and out over the desolate southwest.

Start out from **La Calera**, at the junction with the La Playa road. Take the stepped alley (CALLE CONTERO) between Bar Parada and the *ayuntamiento* (town hall), then the first steps on the right. At the top of the steps turn right along a narrow alley between houses, then turn left when you meet a road higher up (on a bend).
Leave this road just beyond a SMALL BRIDGE and above a large WATER TANK: a SIGN FOR THE **GR 132** marks the start of the walk proper (**10min**). Take steps left uphill beside the *barranco* and swing left almost immediately to cross it. Your ascent of the towering cliffs has begun. This initial stretch of

path, on well-graded zigzags, is paved in places, but sometimes very gravelly with loose grit and small stones. From here on, always follow the main red and white waymarked GR, ignoring any turn-offs.
As you climb, banana plantations, a deep blue sea, and dark bluffs come into view below — followed by a glimpse of the small *barrios* (urban districts) occupying the highest corner of the valley, a shrill patch of greenery in these monochromatic surroundings. The island you can see looking back across the sea, more than likely under cloud, is El Hierro.
A solid slog lasting well over an hour brings you to a ridge

(**Riscos de la Mérica**), from where you look straight down onto La Playa and Vueltas (Valle Gran Rey's port area). This setting is dramatised by the jagged ridges tumbling down alongside you. Later you reach the CREST (**1h45min**), where goats graze on the remains of terracing. Once you are above the end of the zigzags, you pass a path off left to the edge of the Riscos — another fine viewpoint.

Ten minutes later you walk between a large RUIN on the left and huge circular THRESHING FLOOR on the right (**1h55min**). Continue up the gently sloping terraces, to catch sight of Arure, set back in a shallow gully on the edge of the plateau. About 15 minutes past the threshing floor you pass to the left of a cistern and another RUINED HOUSE by a cluster of rocks. The country villages of Chipude, El Cercado and Las Hayas (from right to left) soon come into view, settings for Walks 12-15.

Five minutes later (**2h15min**) you pass a path forking left to the trig point at the summit of **La Mérica**. You cross over a neck of ridge and now briefly catch a view northwest, towards a formidable landscape of bare rock, devoid of life and drained of colour … the perfect site for a rubbish tip! La Palma lies before you, two rounded peaks emerging above a cape of lingering cloud.

On reaching a track (**2h35min**), continue along it, ignoring the turn-off left to the rubbish tip a few minutes later. Less than 20 minutes along the track, ignore a path on the left signposted to Taguluche (the return route for Walk 11). Just beyond the turn-off, you're gazing down onto Taguluche — a patchwork of gardens in a tremendously deep basin.

Having crossed the ridge a few times, you descend to a tarmac lane. Follow this for 100m/yds, then turn left on a cobbled path to the **Mirador and Ermita del Santo** (**3h10min**; Picnic 10), a magnificent viewpoint overlooking the Taguluche ravine and the setting for Walk 11 — which descends from here to Taguluche.

From the *mirador,* go back to the lane junction and turn left to the main road. Head left uphill to the friendly BAR CONCHITA in **Arure**. Or walk downhill to the BAR/RESTAURANT EL JAPE. In either case you'll reach a BUS STOP (**3h15min**).

About 15 minutes past the threshing floor you pass to the left of a cistern and another ruined house by a cluster of rocks. In spring the landscape is bright with tree-spurge (Euphorbia dendroides).

See map pages 70-71
Distance: 9.5km/6mi; 4h
Grade: very strenuous —
especially the return ascent of
700m/2300ft. The long descent
of 700m follows gravelly and
slippery paths at times, some of
which are vertiginous; you must
be sure-footed and have a head
for heights. Only attempt in
good weather. Part of the walk is
waymarked red/white (GR 132).
Important note: Several maps
and guides feature a footpath in
the Barranco de Guaranet north
of Taguluche (called Barranco de
Guariñén on the Cabildo map).
This path *should be avoided:* it is
in extremely poor condition and
will no longer be maintained by
the government, as it is no
longer one of their 40 recommended walks (see page 37).
Equipment: walking boots,
walking stick(s), fleece, windproof, long trousers, whistle,
sunhat, picnic, plenty of water
Access: 🚌 or 🚐 (Timetables
11, 16) to Arure. By car, park
opposite Bar Conchita in the
centre. By bus, alight at the
Bar/Restaurant El Jape.
**Alternative walk: Arure —
Ermita San Salvador —
Taguluche — Arure** (7km/
4.3mi; 3h45min). Very strenuous, with a skiddy descent of
500m/1600ft down a steep,
gravelly path. This difficult trail
is No 8 in the Cabildo's list of
recommended walks, so the path
will presumably be maintained.
While not enjoying this tedious
descent ourselves, we include it
for sure-footed, adventurous hikers.

*Only suitable in fine, dry weather
(danger of rockfall).* Equipment/
access as above. Start out as for
the main walk, but turn off left
50m/yds beyond the **Mirador
Ermita del Santo** (where the
main walk continues to the
right). Follow this narrow,
skiddy path down the face of the
escarpment, sometimes on steep
steps. Some 30min below the
mirador, the way is cairned: you
pass just to the left of a strip of
trees, scrambling through
brambles. Ten minutes later the
path goes straight down the
ridge. Lower down, past a row
of houses, you may come to an
old sign, 'MONUMENTO NATURAL
LOMO DE CARRETON' (**1h05min**).
Keep right at the fork here, then
join a road and follow it downhill. At the T-junction ahead,
cross straight over the road onto
a rough, rocky path (barely
visible at the outset). It takes you
down to a bend in the main road
in **Taguluche**. Follow the path
straight over the road, keeping
to the right of the houses just
below the road. On meeting the
end of a road, turn left to pick
up the continuing path (down
concrete steps). Pass the end of a
road, then circle to the right of a
TRANSFORMER STATION
(**1h25min**). At a fork five
minutes later, turn right to the
main road and follow it uphill. A
good five minutes up the road,
take the seconding turning left
(an asphalt road) to the **Ermita
San Salvador** (**1h35min**; Picnic
11). Pick up the main walk here
at the 2h30min-point.

I f you like challenging hikes in barren and impressive
landscapes, then this is the walk for you! The terrain is
rugged and harsh, but the scenery is spectacular. The route
starts off along 'cliff-hanging' paths, and the homeward
stretch is a marvel — the path coils its way up a sheer valley
wall, yet never once is it vertiginous.

Taguluche, from the 2h30min-point in the walk. The Ermita San Salvador is the lone building in the centre background.

Start out in **Arure**. If you come by car, from BAR CONCHITA walk 500m/yds downhill towards Valle Gran Rey, to a hairpin bend in the main road, where you can turn right for the MIRADOR ERMITA DEL SANTO. If you come by bus, alight at the bus stop outside the BAR/ RESTAURANT EL JAPE and follow the main road towards the centre of Arure, passing the Las Hayas turn-off. Then take the first left turn off the hairpin bend for the MIRADOR ERMITA DEL SANTO. After 100m/yds turn right to climb a paved walkway, the red- and white-waymarked **GR 132**, to the **Mirador Ermita del Santo**. From here, the dramatic setting of Taguluche, 500m/1650ft below, sets the mood for the hike. Take your bearings here: you will head along the escarpment to the right and then descend, to circle in front of the razor-like ridge on the right side of the valley — at the end of which lies the Chapel of San Salvador. The return route is up the left wall of the Taguluche Valley.

Still keen? Set off on the GR path behind the *ermita* and, after 50m/yds, keep right at a Y-fork *(the Alternative walk goes left here)*. Make your way through a light scattering of pines, to edge along the escarpment. The views are stupendous — for those sure enough of foot to enjoy them. A very steep descent (initially on a stone-paved path) follows but, some 20 minutes from the *mirador*, a section of path, below vertical rock walls, is very loose underfoot, narrow and vertiginous.

You reach the edge of a VAST BASIN (**40min**), looking down on the large farming settlement of Alojera. The heights, benefiting from the trade winds, are noticeably greener than the lower hills, some of which are totally bare.

Another slippery, gravelly descent drops you down over the ridge towards the Taguluche road. Just before you reach the road, turn left at a fork (**1h**), *leaving* the GR 132 which continues on the far side of the road to Alojera. The well-kept path overlooks the desolate and inhospitable **Barranco de**

75

Guaranet. (Originally this walk approached Taguluche via the Guaranet *barranco*, but the path has deteriorated badly in recent years — extremely narrow and exposed, in some places it's almost invisible; since it is not on the Cabildo's list of recommended walks, it is unlikely ever to be repaired.)

Five minutes along you cross a crest — to find the tiny settlement of Taguluche now lying at your feet in the depth of the next *barranco*. The path is lined with *Euphorbia*, wild flowers and agaves.

When you reach the Taguluche road, cross it and pick up the downhill trail again (10m/yds to the left and cairn-marked). Meet the end of a road near a small CEMETERY and cross it to continue downhill. When you come to a WATERCOURSE (**1h20min**), walk along the right-hand side for a minute, then cross over to the left side

and walk uphill. Just before you reach the main road (by a water deposit), pick up an old track and follow it to the right. Soon it becomes a path and turns right downhill through an old palm grove, back to the road. Now follow the road to the right, downhill. At the next junction turn right uphill to the pretty **Ermita San Salvador**. (**1h50min**; Picnic 11), where you can enjoy a break in the shade.

Setting off again, walk back to the junction with the main road and now turn right. Ignore a road to the right just past Bar Taguluche. In 10 minutes you reach a TURNING AREA at the end of the road (**2h05min**). (Steps from this turning area lead into a paved path which descends to some houses after 10 minutes. There used to be a path from the houses to the viewpoint shown in the small photo opposite, but it was been closed off by the

landowners some years ago. We notice that the path is shown on the Cabildo map as part of route No 8. This is likely to be a mistake — and we did not have time to investigate during the latest research — but you might like to see if it has been reopened.

From the turning area go back along the road for about 20m/yds, then climb steps on the right, which leads into an old trail. Barely a minute up (just past the last house), turn left on a narrow path climbing the hillside (WHITE ARROW). A couple of minutes up, the old path becomes clearer. A good five minutes from the road, you cross a three-way water pipe and continue straight up the hillside, ignoring the paths left and right. You're overlooking Taguluche, which clings to the ridge opposite. Small garden plots, green and fertile, occupy most of the ridge, with a mixture of mango, avocado, fig, citrus trees and an abundance of palms.

The path is now clearly defined and marked with occasional cairns.

The path crosses to the left of the valley floor (**2h30min**); 50m/yds further on, ignore a path to the left. On the outskirts of **Taguluche**, ascend through abandoned terracing, after 15 minutes ignoring a path to the right. With the ascent nearly over (**3h30min**), go through a passage in the ridge top — to overlook an abyss. A minute later, the path loops up below a goat's pen. Ten minutes further uphill, join a track and turn left (this is the red/white waymarked **GR 132**). After 10 more minutes, pass the turn-off to the Mirador Ermita del Santo and reach the road in **Arure**. Turn right to the BUS STOP outside the BAR/RESTAURANT EL JAPE — or turn left if you've parked near the BAR CONCHITA (**4h**).

Left: cultivated fields in springtime, near the watercourse crossed at the 1h20min-point in the walk.
Below: view to the old port at Punta de Pejereyes. Unfortunately, the path to this viewpoint had been closed off by landowners the last time we looked (see text at the 2h05min-point).

See map pages 70-71
Distance: 8.7km/5.5mi; 3h
Grade: relatively easy, with an ascent of 100m/330ft and an overall descent of 900m/3000ft. But the final 400m/1300ft descent to Los Granados is tough on the knees. Waymarked from Las Hayas (partly GR 131)
Equipment: walking boots, walking stick(s), sunhat, fleece, windproof, raingear, picnic, water
Access: 🚐 to the Bar/Restaurant El Jape in Arure (Timetables 11, 16); journey time from Valle Gran Rey 35min. Return on the same bus from Los Granados; journey time 10min to Valle Gran Rey
Short walks
1 **Las Hayas — Los Granados** (4.7km/3mi; 1h55min). Grade (descent) and equipment as above. Access: 🚐 (Timetables 11, 14, 16) to La Montaña Restaurant at Las Hayas; journey time 50min. Follow the main walk from the 1h05min-point to the end.
2 **Las Hayas — Jardín de las Creces — Las Hayas** (5.4km/3.3mi; 1h15min). Easy, with an ascent/descent of only about 60m/200ft. This is a little gem of a circuit in a centuries-old,

untouched laurel forest. Equipment as main walk.
Access: 🚗 or 🚐 (as for Short walk 1) to La Montaña restaurant (described on page 25). From the RESTAURANT, walk east uphill on the main road. In the first curve, turn left on the **GR 131**; red/white waymarks). You pass to the left of the village CHURCH (**5min**), then turn left at a fork and enter the **Garajonay National Park** (signpost after 20m/yds). At a junction 30m/yds past the sign, keep half right and pass through a wind-sculpted part of the laurel forest, with trees covered with moss and dripping with lichen. Reaching a wide forestry track with a signpost 'CARRETERA DORSAL' (**15min**), fork right. In 20min you pass through the little **Jardín de las Creces** picnic area. Now *leave* the GR 131: take the first path to the left (by a 'LAS CRECES' sign), along a small fern-covered gully. This path is one of the self-guided routes in the national park. At a junction 20 minutes after leaving the GR 131, keep left; some 15min later you arrive back at the junction with the CARRETERA DORSAL. Cross this track and retrace your steps to **Las Hayas**.

F ew walks on this island are without their ups and downs, and most have at least one vertiginous section. Unusually, this walk has no long uphill slog, and the vertiginous stretches can be avoided. The gentle climb through a fragment of the laurel wood and the spectacular descent into Valle Gran Rey make this a superb easy hike.

Start out at the BAR/RESTAURANT EL JAPE: continue along the road towards **Arure**. But just around the bend in the road, fork right towards Las Hayas. Arure is strung out along the far wall of the valley, while the floor of the *barranco* is crammed with vegetable gardens. A good five

minutes uphill, leave the road just above a SMALL RESERVOIR: take the path down to and alongside the dam wall. Beyond the dam wall turn right at the fork. Once past the houses above the dam, follow the path up to the left (northeast) over a rocky ridge; small cairns mark the route. The ridge is covered in yellow-flowering *Tecina linifolia Gomerae*.

Crossing the crest, a view opens up over an elevated valley. The path, rich in mauve, pink, and terracotta hues, joins a track and curves to the right. Tarmac comes under foot at the first house, the lane passes above a SECOND RESERVOIR (**30min**). At a T-JUNCTION (**35min**) turn right, and at the following Y-fork (where there are many signs) turn right again for 'LAS CRECES', climbing into a basin full of vineyards.

At the next fork, keep right for . 'LAS HAYAS'. Follow the tarred lane uphill until it ends just above a stream bed (**40min**). Cross the *barranco* and ascend a path into a patch of laurel wood. Meeting another road (**50min**),

Lomo del Balo, as seen on the approach to Los Descansaderos

turn left. Keeping to the crest of the ridge (**Cabezo de la Vizcaína**), ignore all turn-offs. As you cut through a crest, Las Hayas comes into view, a small scattering of houses surrounded by heather and laurel woods. Approaching the village, a road joins from the right. Five minutes later, just before the main road in **Las Hayas**, go half left uphill on a track and then turn right on a lane, to emerge facing the MONTAÑA restaurant (**1h05min**), described on page 25.

From the restaurant, return to the main road, and immediately turn sharp left on a lane (**GR 131**; red and white waymarks). This leads down into a valley of palm trees, crosses a *barranco* and then rises gently. Coming over a low crest, you meet a crossing road (**1h15min**): go straight over but, 25m/yds further downhill, turn left on the GR 131 and begin to descend into another valley of palms. Then, at a Y-fork 50m/yds further on, turn right for 'LA VISCAÍNA' (the GR 131 continues ahead to El Cercado). Cross a track to continue into the valley and, on the far side, at a junction beyond another low crest, go right— to

overlook an abyss, the **Barranco del Agua**, a tributary of the Barranco Valle Gran Rey. From here you can make out the line of a path ascending the valley wall opposite; it climbs to El Cercado and is the route of Walk 14. La Fortaleza, the table-topped rock shown on page 31, sits in the background. Soon the striking grandeur of Valle Gran Rey, a luxuriant tapestry of banana groves, cane and vegetable gardens, comes into view. A small *mirador* with a stone bench makes a fine picnic spot (Picnic 12).

Coming onto cobbles (**1h 30min**), you now begin a *very steep* descent down a zigzag path; it's a fine piece of workmanship, and not at all vert whole length of the valley lies in view. Cross a small watercourse and keep left at a fork just beyond it, to step down to a road in **Los Descansaderos** (**2h30min**). Turn left down the palm-flooded valley floor. Keep to this road all the way to the Valle Gran Rey road, ignoring the side road forking to the left. When you reach the main road at **Los Granados** (**3h**), descend to the BUS STOP, a minute downhill to the left.

Valle Gran Rey, from near the setting for Picnic 12

Walk 13: CHIPUDE • ERMITA NUESTRA SEÑORA DE GUADALUPE • VALLE GRAN REY

See map pages 70-71
Distance: 8.5km/5.5mi; 3h25min
Grade: moderate-strenuous, with a descent of 1000m/3300ft. You must be sure-footed and have a head for heights. The descent into Valle Gran Rey is very slippery, so don't attempt the walk in wet weather.
Equipment: walking boots, walking stick(s), fleece, windproof, sunhat, raingear, picnic, water
Access: 🚌 to Chipude (Timetables 11, 14, 16); journey time from Valle Gran Rey 1h. Or 🚗: Park in Chipude off the plaza and return by bus to your car (Timetables 11, 16).
Important note: We used to describe an Alternative walk (for experts) from Valle Gran Rey up the Barranco de Argaga to Nuestra Señora de Guadalupe, but there have now been several accidents, deaths and rock-falls on this route. We do not think it would be responsible to include it in the present or future editions — the route will not be maintained, since it is not one of the Cabildo's 40 recommended routes.
Short walk: Chipude — Ermita Nuestra Señora de Guadalupe — El Cercado — Chipude (7,9km/ 4.9mi; 2h45min). A relatively easy circular walk, with a descent/ re-ascent of 300m/1000ft. You must be sure-footed and have a head for heights. Access, equipment as main walk. Follow the main walk to the **Ermita Nuestra Señora de Guadalupe**, then return to the signposted 40min-point in the main walk (**1h40min**). Turn left uphill here on a path signposted for 'EL CERCADO'. Notice the rocks: on the opposite site of the *barranco* they are covered with white lichen because of the influence and the direction of the wet trade winds, while on the other side of the barranco they are black, protected from these prevailing winds. After some 20 minutes uphill from the valley floor the trail enters a side-arm of the valley. El Cercado is now visible on the top. You pass through prickly pear, agaves and many abandoned terraces. Higher up the path is lined with small white rock roses *(Cistus)*. Some 10 minutes later, when the path forks above cultivated fields, keep left. Coming to a road in another five minutes, turn left; then, 10m/yds further on, turn right on the signposted **GR 131** for 'CHIPUDE' (**2h20min**). Turn right for 100m/yds, then climb the red/white waymarked GR to the left. Cross the main road and climb the ridge above. When you cross a track, descend the hillside on the same path. Chipude lies across the valley. Go over the road once more, and then cross a shallow valley. Rejoining the road, this time follow it to the right, into **Chipude** (**2h45min**) and return to your car or pick up a bus.

Leaving Chipude, the highest village on the island (1050m/3450ft), you may well set off in a playful mist; it creeps down on you, then disperses in wisps, revealing picture-postcard views. The walk winds its way through two quiet green valleys before making a dramatic descent into Valle Gran Rey.

Setting out from the CHURCH in **Chipude**, cross the road to BAR LA CANDELARIA, and descend the lane at the right of the bar (initially cobbled, but it quickly becomes tarred). On reaching the road to El Cercado, turn left. After 25m/yds, turn right down another signposted road. When the road forks after some 50m/yds, keep right. At the end of the road, take steps which descend to a house on the right. Then turn left immediately on a trail with street lights. Leaving the last of the houses behind, descend into the valley.

Soon meeting a TRACK (**10min**), turn left and then immediately right. Fig trees abound in this valley, with its grassy walls. After a few minutes keep left at a fork. Large tracts of prickly pear cover the *barranco* walls, suggesting earlier cultivation. Twenty minutes from the track, keep an eye out for your turn-off — go sharp right at the fork here

(**30min**), to continue on the main trail which heads left down into the valley. In about 10 minutes, you arrive at the BED OF THE **Barranco de la Matanza** (**40min**), where you join a trail coming down from El Cercado. (*This trail is the return route for the Short walk.*)

Almost straight ahead a trail drops very steeply down towards La Vizcaína; it's worth enjoying the fantastic view at the start of that path. But the main walk continues to the left (past the lone palm tree), following the left-hand side of the **Barranco de Argaga**. An unused *canal* in varying stages of collapse will keep you company all the way to the Ermita Nuestra Señora de Guadalupe. Most of the time you're walking alongside it on a clear path, sometimes — for very short stretches — you're walking within it. In winter, pretty pools fill the *barranco* bed. A mass of stone walls covers the sides of the valley. The *ermita* comes into sight ahead, sitting on a protruding ridge. Coming into a corner of the *barranco* full of fruit trees, vegetable plots and vines, scramble over and around the broken *canal*, to cross a side *barranco* (**50min**).

Here you need to identify the route you'll be taking after visiting the *ermita*. During the next 15 minutes it lies in view: it is the lower and clearer of two paths ascending the valley wall opposite. Take note, too, of the cobbled trail that crosses the canal and descends into the valley, to join this lower path — it's the red and white waymarked GR 132, your ongoing route. But first visit the chapel, five minutes further along the *canal*

The Ermita Nuestra Señora de Guadalupe, seen from above Gerián

Spring landscape, some 15 minutes into the walk from Chipude

— the **Ermita Nuestra Señora de Guadalupe** (sometimes called Guará; **1h10min**). The chapel's balcony-like perch offers a superb view, looking down into the Barranco de Argaga as it twists and winds its way seaward. *(The Short walk returns to Chipude from here.)*

Return to the crossing with the **GR 132** and descend left to the valley floor. The cobbled trail crosses the stream bed and then turns back to the left. At a fork higher up, keep left. Ascending to the pass, you look down into the emerald-green pools of the *barranco* bed.

Crossing the signposted pass (**Degollada del Cerrillal; 1h40min**), keep *right*. (Do not continue along the crest to the left.) Start to descend into Valle Gran Rey. An impressive view greets you straight away, and more views unfold on the descent — of severe, charred-brown ravine walls that seal off the valley. The downhill path is initially in good shape, but further down steep and gravelly — extremely slippery! *Descend with care!* The enormity of the valley is evident minutes later, when you peer down onto its

upper reaches over a mosaic of vivid green plots and palm trees layering the floor, set off by bright-white dwellings. On the descent you pass a makeshift GOATS' PEN (**2h**).

The path twirls steeply downhill, and the rest of the valley opens up. Curling up and over a rocky ridge, you come to two forks: go right at the first one, then, half a minute later, keep left at the next, on a wide cobbled trail. Just after crossing a stream bed, pass two rustic cottages with colourful gardens (**2h40min**). Turn left at the junction below them, making for another chapel, the Ermita de los Reyes. Keep downhill on the main path. Cross the courtyard of the **Ermita de los Reyes** (**2h45min**) and descend steps on the right. Now you can either follow the GR 132 across the *barranco* and up to the main road in **El Guro** (**2h55min**; BUS STOP) or turn left and take the track down alongside the *barranco*. Leave the *barranco* before getting to the municipal dump, and head up to the road. This takes you to the BUS STATION at La Calera in **Valle Gran Rey** (**3h25min**).

Walk 14: LOMO DEL BALO • LA VIZCAINA • CHIPUDE • LA FORTALEZA • CHIPUDE

See map pages 70-71; see photographs pages 31, 79
Distance: 10km/6mi; 4h15min
Grade: strenuous, with an overall ascent of 700m/2300ft (of which 600m/2000ft at the outset). You must be sure-footed and have a head for heights. The ascent of La Fortaleza, a vertiginous and potentially dangerous scramble, is only for very experienced hikers. Only attempt in fine weather.
Equipment: walking boots, walking stick(s), sunhat, fleece, windproof, raingear, picnic, water
Access: 🚌 to Lomo del Balo at the end of Valle Gran Rey (Timetables 11, 16); journey from Valle Gran Rey 15 min.

To return: 🚌 from Chipude (Timetables 11, 14, 16); journey time to Valle Gran Rey 1h
Short walks
1   Lomo del Balo — La Vizcaína — El Cercado — Chipude (5.2km/3.3mi; 2h20min). Equipment/access/grade as above (ascent of 500m/1650ft). Follow the main walk to Chipude; omit La Fortaleza.
2   Chipude — La Fortaleza — Chipude (4.7km/3mi; 1h55min). The overall ascent is only 160m/500ft, but see under 'Grade' above). Equipment as above. 🚗 or 🚌 (Timetables 11, 14, 16) to/from Chipude; journey time from Valle Gran Rey 1h. Follow the main walk from the 2h20min-point.

L a Fortaleza is everything a real mountain should be: a struggle to the top and superb views when you get there — just the ticket for the adventurous. In contrast, Short walk 1 avoids the difficulties of the mountain ascent and makes a superb evening walk, under the setting sun.

Leave the bus at **Lomo del Balo**, at the TURN-OFF FOR LA VIZCAINA. **Set off** by following the road round the end of the valley to two stepped hamlets, **Los Descansaderos** and then **La Vizcaína** (20min). Just before house No 71, take the stepped and cobbled path ascending from the parking bay (INFORMATION BOARD and signpost for 'EL CERCADO'). Keep left and walk straight uphill, looking across a lush palm-studded corner of the valley. After a few minutes, ignore a path to the left. Now the cliffs rise straight up in front of you.
Soon you cross a WATER CHANNEL. Ignore the minor paths to the right; you will stay on this main trail all the way to the village of El Cercado. Prickly pear, broom, and *tabaiba* grow

out of the hillside rock. The trail, a magnificent piece of workmanship, winds its way up the valley wall, from one ledge to another. Ignore a trail off right (**50min**): it is a very difficult, potentially dangerous ascent. Partridges may startle you, as your passage flushes them out of the bushes. The *barranco* soon closes into a narrow defile.
The trail leaves the valley and mounts a CREST (**1h40min**). Now walking along the very edge of the valley wall, a spectacular view is revealed down to the left. El Cercado comes into sight, its houses sprinkled around a basin. Go straight up the road to the main road in **El Cercado** (**1h50min**). Turn right and after 40m/yds reach the BAR/RESTAURANT VICTORIA, a friendly place with good food.

Descend the concrete path opposite, below the road, heading left and meandering through this sleepy farming village. On reaching a small road, turn right for 100m/yds, then climb the red/white waymarked **GR 131** to the left. Cross the main road and climb the ridge above. When you cross a track, descend the hillside on the same path. Chipude lies across the valley. Go over the road once more, and then cross a shallow valley. Rejoining the road, this time follow it to the right, into **Chipude**. Notice the communal LAUNDRY PLACE (Lavaderos 'La Vica') below the road. Three minutes later, cross the road and climb the path at the left of the BUS SHELTER, up to the CHURCH (**2h20min**). *(Short walk 1 ends here, and Short walk 2 begins here.)*

Now follow the road uphill towards San Sebastián for some 150m/yds, then ascend the cobbled trail to the left (still the **GR 131**). Cross the main road on the crest above, then continue on the trail to the left of the BUS SHELTER. La Fortaleza now looms up ahead. After a minute, you reach the ROAD TO LA DAMA. Turn left and, after 50m/yds, pick up the trail again. Cross another crest and rejoin the same road in the village of **El Apartadero**. Turn left and walk 200m/yds to the BAR CAMIONEROS. Descend the trail opposite the bar into the valley below, clad in prickly pear cacti.

Rejoining the road (**2h40min**), turn left. After 50m/yds, turn right to ascend a concrete lane into the little hamlet of **Pavón**. From the end of the lane the path, flanked by small vineyards, goes right, up the V in the hillside. About three minutes uphill, at a junction by a a beautifully

renovated TRADITIONAL HOUSE, turn right on the path to La Fortaleza (*leaving* the GR 131, which heads left towards Garajonay). Half a minute up you're on the very edge of the plunging **Barranco de Erque** (Picnic 14). Now for the assault. Head up the path; the scramble begins at the foot of this buttress, and soon you head up a ROCK CREVICE. *Great care is needed;* the path is well worn, stepped in places, but very steep and awkward. This hair-raising stretch only lasts a couple of minutes, but please note, *it is potentially dangerous!*

Above the crevice, the rock faces fall away on either side of you. Now clamber over a narrow neck of rock towards the table-topped summit. *Taking great care not to venture too close to the edge,* circle to the right, to reach a CROSS ON THE SUMMIT PLATEAU of **La Fortaleza** (**3h10min**). You are greeted by a magnificent vista across the southwestern corner of the island, where the villages you passed earlier lie just below. The TRIG POINT (1232m/ 4041ft) lies a few minutes further round. The large plantation you can see on the edge of plateau, high above the sea, is La Dama. The views to the east, over the deeply-gouged Barranco de Erque, will leave you in awe.

Allow 20min to circle the table-top. Back at the ROCK CREVICE, return the same way to **Chipude** (**4h15min**), where the bus stops outside BAR LA CANDELARIA. (Or return to the junction by the renovated house and follow the GR 131 to the right for 10 minutes, with grand views over the *barranco*. Meeting the road to Erque, turn left and in 10 more minutes rise to the main road, where you can hail a bus.)

Walk 15: CRUCE DE LA ZARCITA • EL CEDRO • GARAJONAY • CHIPUDE

Map begins on pages 112-113, continues on pages 96-97 and ends on pages 70-71; see also photographs on pages 1, 2, 117

Distance: 13.5km/8.5mi; 4h35min

Grade: fairly strenuous, especially on the 650m/2100ft ascent from El Cedro to Garajonay. Best done on a fine settled day (weather conditions in this part of the island change rapidly).

Equipment: walking boots and stick(s), sunhat, fleece, windproof, raingear, picnic, water

Access: 🚌 to Cruce de la Zarcita (Timetable 11); journey time from Valle Gran Rey 1h25min. Or 🚗 car to the El Cedro turn-off north of Cruce de la Zarcita (room for a few cars).
To return: 🚌 from Chipude (Timetables 11, 14, 16); journey time to Valle Gran Rey 1h. Or 🚗 taxi back to your car (taxi service from Bar Sonia, opposite Bar Candelaria in Chipude).

Short walks

1 Las Mimbreras — Los Aceviños forestry track — El Cedro — Ermita Nuestra Señora de Lourdes — Las Mimbreras (6km/3.5mi; 1h45min). Easy, except for a steep and slippery 15min descent to El Cedro. Equipment as above. Access by 🚗: turn down the El Cedro road (Car tour 5 at 103km, page 29) and take the first left turn (after 1.5km: this is

the Los Aceviños forestry track and is signposted 'Arroyo de El Cedro'). There is a parking area 1.8km further on at Las Mimbreras. Start out by continuing along the track towards LOS ACEVIÑOS (signposted). After 40 minutes turn right on a path signposted 'CASERIO EL CEDRO'. Just 40m/yds downhill turn right on another path and a minute later turn right again. When you reach a junction of tarred lanes in 15 minutes, go straight across to continue downhill to the restaurant LA VISTA. Then descend concrete steps to the left of the restaurant. Turn right along the path below the camping area and, in two minutes, cross the stream and turn left up a road (**1h10min**). Then turn right at the first junction for 'LAS MIMBRERAS', to pick up the main walk at the 55min-point. Follow the main walk back to the car park.

2 Alto del Contadero — Garajonay summit — Alto del Contadero (2.5km/1.5mi; 40min). Moderate, with an ascent/descent of 250m/800ft. Stout shoes will suffice. Access by 🚗: park at roadside parking area at Alto del Contadero, where the beautiful stone-laid Garajonay forestry track leaves the main road (nearest 🚌 stop: Pajarito). Follow the main walk from the 2h40min-point, to the summit; return the same way.

Garajonay, the island's highest summit (1487m/4877ft), spends much of the year veiled in cloud and mist, accounting for La Gomera's abundant water supply and providing the ideal environment for the *Laurisilva* forest. This hike begins in this cool damp forest, walking alongside and over a stream. From Garajonay, you'll have a 360° panorama across the island's wooded hub and, heading home, you'll cross farmed slopes in a quiet, rarely visited valley.

Set off from **Cruce de la Zarcita**: continue along the road towards Hermigua. Just 20m/yds from the junction, leave the road for the second path on the right, signposted to 'REVENTON OSCURO' and 'EL CEDRO'. It gives you fine views back to Los Roques. Meeting the road again after 20 minutes, cross straight over on a cobbled road signposted 'CASERIO DE EL CEDRO'. After 20 minutes, as the road describes a hairpin bend to the left (**40min**), you'll see three paths forking off to the right. Descend the path furthest to the left here. Five minutes downhill, the path leads into a large parking area behind the AULA DE LA NATURALEZA. Descend the steps into the grounds, then turn right to pick up the path. Stay to the right of the buildings, then follow a steep path alongside a fence. This takes you back to the (now concreted) road, which you follow downhill. A few minutes later, just above the valley floor, a view unfolds across to El Cedro, set on a hillside of terraced gardens. This small pocket of cultivation is virtually swallowed up by the encircling hills wooded in *Laurisilva*.

You reach a junction (**55min**). *(Short walk 1 joins here.)* Turn left and, at the next junction, turn left again (signposted to 'LAS MIMBRERAS'). Some three-four minutes later, take the first left turn, climbing a wide stone-laid path with steps. Ascending the valley wall, you pass several side paths; keep to the widest and clearest all the way, passing some houses. On reaching the 'PARQUE NACIONAL GARAJONAY' sign, you enter the forest (and the national park). A shady path with tall spindly trees coated in moss leads you up to a small

Nuestra Señora de Lourdes

rustic chapel, **Nuestra Señora de Lourdes** (**1h20min**). Beyond the picnic area and chapel, a small wooden bridge takes you over the stream and deeper into the forest. Cross another bridge and climb to a forestry track. Turn right and, after some 50m/yds, turn left on a path signposted 'EL CONTADERO/ALTO DE GARAJONAY'. After five minutes the way forks. Keep left and, when the fork to the right rejoins your path ten minutes further uphill (after crossing the river bed twice), keep left again. Climbing steadily, you come to a small viewpoint looking out to Roque de Agando and El Teide on Tenerife. As you rise higher, tree heather is the dominant vegetation.

Finally you emerge on the Laguna Grande road at **Alto del Contadero** (**2h45min**). *(Short walk 2 begins here.)* Cross the road and head up the beautiful stone-laid forestry track opposite (sign: 'ALTO DE GARAJONAY'). Remain on this track all the way to the top. Weather permitting, you will enjoy a splendid view from the **Garajonay** SUMMIT (**3h05min**; Picnic 15) over the undulating hills of the plateau. Chipude can be seen to the west.

Leaving the mountain, go down to the track behind the summit

viewpoint (keeping right at a fork almost at once) and descend for five minutes on the pretty track you came up on. Then turn left at a junction (sign: 'CHIPUDE'). A couple of minutes later go half-right on another stone-laid track. A steep descent follows, during which you ignore a track to the left. *Now referring to the map on pages 70-71,* eventually you encounter two junctions in close succession. Go left at the first (next to a small pine wood; **3h35min**) but, at the second, take a path entering the scrub *between* the right and left forks. This becomes a track and forks after two minutes; turn right here, downhill (sign: 'CHIPUDE'). Remain on this old trail — washed out in places and overgrown with a profusion of wild flowers in spring (see photograph). The descent is through a valley patched in vineyards. Rounding the hillside, drop down to the hamlet of **Los Manantiales (4h10min)** and cross a road. Follow the trail to the right. Just past the first building, follow the path sharp left. Stepping down to a crossing path, turn left and, 50m/yds further on (below a house), descend the second path on the right. This steep cobbled trail crosses the *barranco*. On the far side the path gently rises along the hillside up to the ridge. Round the valley above vineyards and when you reach the first houses, turn right on a cobbled lane. Follow this down to the main road in **Chipude (4h35min)**, by the PLAZA, BAR LA CANDELARIA and BUS STOP.

Top and middle: descending to Los Manantiales; bottom: the cumbre *is often swallowed up in clouds carried by the trade winds.*

Walk 16: EL RUMBAZO • (TARGA) • PLAYA DE SANTIAGO

See map pages 96-97; see also photograph page 92

Distance: 10.2km/6.5mi; 3h55min

Grade: very steep and strenuous initial ascent of 500m/1650ft (best done on an overcast day); the rest is easy. The path is amply wide (see photo), but you must be sure-footed and have a head for heights. Don't attempt in wet or windy weather. The trails are signposted.

Equipment: walking boots, sunhat, fleece, raingear, picnic, plenty of water

Access: 🚕 taxi (or with friends) from Playa de Santiago to the El Rumbazo turn-off beyond Taco (on the road to Pastrana)
To return: 🚐 (Timetables 13, 17) or ⛴ (Timetable 18) from Playa de Santiago

Short walks

1 El Rumbazo — Targa (2.3km/1.4mi; 1h30min). Grade (ascent), equipment and access as above. Return by 🚐 from the Targa turn-off to Playa de Santiago (Timetables 13, 16); journey time 15min. Follow the main walk to the road on the PASS by Targa (**1h25min**). Turn right on the road, then walk to the main road and BUS STOP.

2 Targa — Playa de Santiago (8km/5mi; 2h20min). Easy descent of 700m/2300ft. Stout shoes will suffice. 🚐 to the Targa turn-off (Timetables 13, 16); journey time from Playa de Santiago 15min. Follow the road into **Targa**, and keep right at the Y-fork after 300m/yds. After another 150m turn right on a path signed 'ANTONCOJO, PLAYA DE SANTIAGO POR GR132'. When the path joins the track, follow the main walk downhill to **Playa de Santiago**.

The amazing and beautiful mountain path that ascends to Targa is one of the most impressive in the Canaries: it is still in immaculate condition, and the precipitous valley wall it climbs will leave you in awe. At times the path seems to hang in mid-air. The route home, by contrast, follows a lazy meandering track down grassy slopes.

Start out at the TURN-OFF TO **El Rumbazo.** Climb the steep road to the hamlet and, at the end of the road, turn sharp right up a trail passing in front of the houses. You look out across the **Barranco de Guarimiar**, teeming with palms. The village set along a hillside shelf over on the right, in the Barranco de Benchijigua, is Pastrana. The prominent finger of rock at the far end of the *barranco* is Roque de Agando, and the hamlet set on the ridge separating the two valleys is El Cabezo.

The beautiful path up to Targa

In the Barranco de Guarimiar, early in the walk; see also photograph page 92.

After a couple of minutes ignore the fork down to a house. Crags of all shapes and sizes rise out of the valley walls above. Gardens burgeoning with produce line the valley floor, although much of the hillside terracing is abandoned.

When you reach a junction by a couple of STONE BUILDINGS (**15min**), turn left (the way ahead continues to Imada). As you climb, looking straight up towards towering overhead cliffs, you'll wonder where on earth your cobbled path goes. On reaching a signposted JUNCTION (**55min**), turn left. (But before doing so, go right for a minute to enjoy a superb view down over the valley from a hillside buttress.)

From here the path (shown on page 89) is vertiginous in places, although amply wide. You cross a *canal* spectacularly engineered in the sheer valley walls. The path winds up from ledge to ledge, clinging to jutting pieces of cliff, with a breathtaking outlook.

Crossing a PASS, you suddenly re-enter civilisation: the pretty little village of **Targa** lies before you when you meet a road (**1h25min**; Picnic 16). A view

90

unfolds across a crescent-shaped grassy shelf of terracing dotted with palms. The rocky outcrops rising out of the valley walls enhance the setting.

Turn left on the road, ignoring all turn-offs and heading for the tall communication MASTS. *(Short walk 1 turns right here.)* In 10 minutes the road takes you to a spectacular viewpoint over Santiago and the airport. These views stay with you as the road reverts to a washed-out track. After 35 minutes on the track, you pass an abandoned homestead on the right and a small reservoir on the left. In the distance you can see the houses of Antoncojo. When the zigzagging ends and the track straightens out, you may encounter a CHAIN BARRIER. Beyond some electricity poles and another abandoned house below you, the track fades somewhat: it veers right, towards the Barranco de la Junta. A few minutes before reaching the main road, the track becomes a tarred lane. Three minutes later, you meet the main road and turn left. Just 100m/yds further on, keep right into **Playa de Santiago** (**3h40min**).

Walk 17: PAJARITO • IMADA • GUARIMIAR • EL RUMBAZO

See map pages 96-97; see also photograph opposite
Distance: 9km/5.6mi; 3h20min
Grade: moderate, with a descent of about 1350m/4400ft, sometimes on gravelly, slippery paths. The descent between Imada and Guarimiar is only recommended for those who are sure-footed and have a head for heights. Don't attempt in wet or windy weather. Well signposted trails.
Equipment: walking boots, walking stick(s), fleece, wind-proof, sunhat, raingear, picnic, water
Access: 🚌 from San Sebastián (Timetable 11); alight at the Pajarito junction; journey time about 35min
To return: 🚕 pre-arranged taxi from the El Rumbazo turn-off (be sure to allow plenty of time to finish the hike). Or walk from the turn-off to Playa de Santiago (4km/2.5mi; 1h) and catch a bus or boat from there.

Short walk: Pajarito — Imada — Alajeró road (7.5km/4.7mi; 2h20min). Moderate, with a descent of 500m/1600ft and an ascent of 200m/650ft. You must be sure-footed and have a head for heights; not suitable in wet or windy weather. Equipment and access as above; return from the Imada turn-off on the Alajeró road to Playa de Santiago (Timetable 13; journey time 20min) and catch a bus from there. Follow the main walk to just over the 1h20min-point, where the main walk descends steps to the left. Just

around the bend in the road, ascend concrete steps on the right, then bear right over rock to locate an old path up to the Alajeró road. Follow the road south for 2km, to the Imada turn-off. *Note:* You could make this walk 20 minutes shorter by alighting from the bus at the turn-off for the 'Caseta de los Noruegos' (also known as 'Casa Olsen' and familiar to most bus drivers). The place is not identified on any sign, but it is a wide, heavily signposted track junction on the south side of the GM2 above El Cedro — 100m east of the KM22 road marker.

Alternative walk: Pajarito — Garajonay — Pajarito — Caseta de los Noruegos — Imada — Guarimiar — El Rumbazo (10.2km/6.5mi; 4h05min). Grade, equipment and access as main walk. Return as main walk. This alternative adds a highly-recommended extension to the start of the main walk. Try to catch a sunrise from the summit of Garajonay! At the crossroads in **Pajarito**, take the track across the road, signposted 'ALTO DE GARAJONAY'. Just into the track, ascend the signposted path to the right, mounting a crest. When a path cuts across in front of you, turn left along it and follow the signs straight along the crest, crossing a small path just before the final climb to the SUMMIT OF **Garajonay** (**25min**). Return the same way to the crossroads in **Pajarito** (**45min**), then follow the main walk described below.

This hike descends all the way from crispy, cool wooded heights. Spice of adventure awaits midway, in the depths of the sheer-sided Barranco de Guarimiar, where a great cliff-hanging but well secured path will leave you in awe.

Start out at **Pajarito**: from the car park on the southeast side of the roundabout follow the track signposted 'LOS ROQUES'. In four minutes, take a path up to the left (the **GR 131**). This trail rises to the main road at a wide, signposted junction (**20min**). Turn sharp right here on the forestry track signposted for 'IMADA'. (The GR continues ahead, after just 50m/yds passing the tiny concrete hut with antennas that has given this area its local name — the CASETA DE LOS NORUEGOS or CASA OLSEN.)

Your track descends through moss-coated laurel woods. You can feel the dampness in the air, as for much of the year these hills are shrouded in cloud, the lifeline of these woods. Exceptionally tall tree heather, dripping with lichen, grows alongside the track.

Out of the trees, the slopes revert to heather, with splashes of pines and eucalyptus. The

In the Barranco de Guarimiar, not far above El Rumbazo. Guarimiar is the hamlet in the background. (See also photograph page 90.)

massive **Barranco de Benchi-jigua**, plunging away on the left, attracts your attention, while the monolithic Roque de Agando bulges up out of the landscape on the far side of the *barranco* (Picnic 17).

Where the track swings right, we reach a small PARKING BAY (**50min**) — a good viewpoint. Benchijigua lies far below in a sprinkling of pines and euca-lyptus. From here take the trail straight ahead. Overgrown vineyards lie almost unnoticed on the rock-rose- and broom-clad valley walls. A good 15 minutes down, ignore the left fork to Azadoe, cross a stream bed with a small seasonal cascade, and then keep right for Imada. The path now runs along the edge of a vertical escarp-ment, where you'll need a head for heights. Rounding the nose of the ridge, you look straight down onto Imada, a biggish farming village sheltering high in the Barranco de Guarimiar. Looking down the *barranco*, you can trace the continuation of your route below the village. Descending to an asphalt road at the upper end of **Imada** (**1h 20min**), continue downhill into the centre and the bar.

From the bar, descend the road to its lowest point, then take the steps descending to the left. (*But for the Short walk, keep to the road, and ascend the concrete steps on the right just around the bend.*) Coming to a fork almost at once, keep right on the lane (left leads to Walk 18) for a few metres, then turn left on a stepped path (SIGNPOST). Keep to the right of the houses. The path narrows and becomes cobbled in places: this is your ongoing route all the way to El Rumbazo. The path descends a bouldery slope in the **Barranco de Guarimiar.**

Terracing covers the slopes all the way up to the rocky crags that line this valley. By the time the *barranco* has folded into a narrow passageway of rock, you reach a rock balcony VIEWPOINT (**2h**). A hamlet lies far below, in a valley liberally sprinkled with palms. From the end of this rocky ledge keep down to the right, to descend the sheer nose of the ridge below you. The path seems to disappear off the end of the ridge, but in fact is built into its side. Stepping down, and very close to the edge, you discover the onward path — a narrow ledge hanging out high above the valley floor, well protected with a rope handrail. No need to worry about turn-offs on this stretch! Heart-beat back to normal, you cross a *canal* built into the valley wall.

Some 20 minutes later you come to some houses in the lush and verdant lower part of **Guarimiar** (**2h35min**). Before the first house, a trail heads down to the stream bed and up to the road into the upper part of the village. Turn left and some 50m/yds further on pick up the stepped path continuing along the right-hand side of the *barranco.* Five minutes or so later, ignore a fork to the right. Further on, you pass by some STONE BUILDINGS (**3h10min**), where the path to the right leads up to Targa (Walk 16).

Under 10 minutes later, you pass above the first house of **El Rumbazo.** The rest of them, a tight cluster, perch on the hillside. Passing in front of them, you join the road and descend to the PLAYA DE SANTIAGO ROAD (**3h20min**), where your taxi should be waiting. If not, Playa de Santiago is under an hour's hike away.

Walk 18: PASTRANA • BENCHIJIGUA • IMADA • ALAJERO ROAD

See map pages 96-97
Distance: 10km/6.2mi; 4h20min

Grade: strenuous, with an overall ascent of 700m/2300ft. You must be sure-footed and have a head for heights. Don't attempt in bad weather. Well signposted trails

Equipment: walking boots, walking stick(s), sunhat, fleece, windproof, raingear, picnic, plenty of water

Access: 🚖 taxi from Playa de Santiago to Pastrana
To return: 🚌 from the Imada turn-off on the Alajeró road (Timetable 13); journey time to Playa de Santiago 20min.

Shorter walk: Roque de Agando — Benchijigua —

View north to Roque de Agando, from the end of the track near the Ermita San Juan (1h30min)

Pastrana (6km/3.5mi; 2h30min). A relatively easy descent of 800m/2600ft. But the first half hour is steep, and pine needles underfoot make it slippery. You must be sure-footed and have a head for heights on a couple of short stretches. Don't attempt in wet weather. Equipment as above. Access by 🚌 to Roque de Agando (Timetable 11); journey time from San Sebastián 35min. For the return, pre-arrange for a taxi (or friends) to meet you in Pastrana, or telephone for a taxi when you arrive there (tel: +34 922 895022). From the FOREST FIRE MEMORIAL at the foot of **Roque de Agando** take the cobbled trail signposted to 'BENCHIJIGUA'. When you reach the 'centre' of **Benchijigua** (a church and a few abandoned houses; **1h05min**), turn left along the motorable track but, after 50m/yds, turn right down a trail. Follow it around the hillside, briefly descending a *barranco* bed and passing below some cottages. Cross another small *barranco* and ascend to a low crest. Turn left and descend to the LO DEL GATO ROAD below (**1h20min**). Follow this road left uphill for about 150m/yds, then pick up your ongoing trail on the right. Follow this (past an old GOFIO MILL on the right) all the way to **Pastrana** (**2h30min**).

Alternative walk: Pastrana — Benchijigua — El Azadoe Pass — El Cabezo — Pastrana (9km/5.6mi; 4h20min). Grade and equipment as main walk (an ascent of 600m/2000ft and descent of 500m/1600ft). You will need to be sure-footed and have a head for heights for the narrow, slippery path between

El Azadoe Pass and the hamlet of El Cabezo. Access: 🚌 to/from Pastrana. Follow the main walk to the **El Azadoe Pass** (**2h40min**). Enjoy the view, then return to the junction just below the pass. Now keep straight ahead (the right-hand fork). Cairns show the way. Ignore all descending paths. At a faint fork above **Guarimiar** (**3h25min**), turn left for EL CABEZO. The path may be a little overgrown, so keep an eye out for the cairns. When you reach **El Cabezo**, descend to a road and turn right. At the next junction turn left. Then turn left on the road to **Pastrana** (**4h**). At the end of the road, just before the ELECTRICITY SUB-STATION, climb a path up to the village. Follow the road back to your car.

T he Barranco de Santiago is not one of those 'love at first sight' ravines. But once beyond its stark and inhospitable façade, the most unexpected sight greets you — a boulder-strewn floor crammed with gardens and orchards. Small hamlets and pretty palms decorate the valley walls, while in winter a stream adds to the beauty. Deeper in among the hills, weird and wonderful rocks burst out of the landscape.

Start out from the TURNING POINT at the end of the road in the picturesque village of **Pastrana**, reached by car or taxi via the upper road from Taco. Take the wide signposted path straight ahead, at the left of the turning point. Pass a few houses and sheds; then, ignoring minor turn-offs, descend into the **Barranco de Benchijigua**. Soon, looking over the stream bed, an enormous bulging pillar of rock high in the V of the *barranco* captures your attention — Roque de Agando. The trail follows either the stream bed or a small path on the left of the bed. After 100m/yds you pass a disused small *molino de gofio** on the left (Picnic 18). At first

glance it looks like a just another small abandoned house, but it is a mill where maize was ground and roasted. About 100m/yds further on, the trail rises to the right, crosses a water pipe and climbs above a large WATER TANK. The ravine gives one final twist, then straightens out to reveal the village of Lo del Gato, set on a terraced hillside adorned with palms. Grassy inclines and a loose scattering of pines give the surrounding hills an alpine aspect.

Where a path forks left to Lo del Gato (**40min**), keep right, continuing straight on around the hillside on a path that is very washed out in places. You cross a watercourse and come to the Lo del Gato road (**1h15min**), where you turn left. After 140m/yds, rejoin your path on the right, ascending the hillside.

Eucalyptus and mimosas welcome you into **Benchijigua**. At a T-junction immersed in prickly pear, turn right. You pass

---

**Gofio* is a popular local food. It's made into a thick paste and mixed with stews and soups or with honey, bananas, almonds, even cheese. The savouries are an acquired taste; the sweets are addictive! Freshly-ground *gofio* is very aromatic.

below some remnants of the village and some charming renovated cottages. Cross a bouldery stream bed and come to a crest with a motorable track, where the **Ermita de San Juan** sits up to the left (**1h30min**). The rocky crest here commands a magnificent view over the village, and indeed the whole valley.

From the ermita walk back under 100m/yds, then turn left and continue past a long building with a 'BENCHIJIGUA' NAMEPLATE: follow the farm track descending behind the chained barrier, signposted for 'IMADA'. Some derelict buildings stand above, with houseleeks and *verode* growing out of their roof tiles. Somewhat over 100m/yds downhill, ignore a fork to the left. Five minutes later, pass some derelict houses. Opposite the last house, where the track descends, turn right on a level path. In early spring the hillsides here are splashed with pink almond blossom. Below you is a small RESERVOIR.

Some 20 minutes from Benchijigua, you cross a crest above some derelict farm buildings. From here the route scales the steep valley wall ahead, keeping near the narrow strip of almond trees on the left-hand side of the escarpment. Continue on the gravelly path around the hillside, then ascend to an overgrown almond orchard and the grassy slopes beyond it. On coming to a T-JUNCTION near the top, turn right. (*A left turn here goes to El Cabezo and is the route of the Alternative walk when returning from the viewpoint at the pass ahead.*) Ascend to **El Azadoe Pass** (**2h40min**), from where you look back over the Benchijigua Valley, an immense

bowl scooped out of the *cumbre*. Over the pass lies a quite different landscape, where greenery is woven into the sheer valley walls. This valley drops down into another, deeper and darker valley, the Barranco de Guarimiar (Walk 17). Just below you sit the remains of the hamlet of El Azadoe, buried in prickly pear.

Your next port of call is Imada, the village you can see a couple of valleys away. Follow the trail down to the right. At a signposted junction a few minutes from Azadoe, keep straight on. On crossing the stream bed, scramble up a rocky slope to the left. Rounding a ridge, you pass above another small hillside outpost and enter the upper reaches of the **Barranco de Guarimiar**, another tributary of the Barranco de Santiago. The valley narrows to a shady passageway, dropping in leaps and bounds. Passing a lone house, descend into the terraced gardens of Imada, embellished with palms. The trail — by now a beautiful stone-laid path — rises to the upper road in **Imada** (**3h25min**), opposite a bar, an ideal refuelling stop.

From the bar, descend the road to its lowest point (where steps on the left lead to Walk 17). Continue round the bend in the road, then climb concrete steps on the right. Up behind the houses, bear right over rock to locate an old path which takes you up to the ALAJERO ROAD in about 25 minutes (**3h50min**). Follow the road south to the TURN-OFF FOR IMADA, where bus line 3 turns round (**4h20min**).

Walk 19: DEGOLLADA DE PERAZA • LA LAJA • ROQUE DE AGANDO • DEGOLLADA DE PERAZA

See map pages 96-97; see also photograph pages 32-33
Distance: 7km/4.5mi; 3h10min
Grade: moderate-strenuous, with an initial descent of 400m/ 1300ft, followed by an ascent of 600m/1970ft. You must be sure-footed and have a head for heights. Don't attempt in wet or windy weather.

Equipment: walking boots, walking stick(s), sunhat, fleece, windproof, raingear, picnic, water
Access: 🚐 to/from the Degollada de Peraza (Timetables 11, 13, 17); journey time from San Sebastián 20min, from Playa de Santiago 1h. Or 🚗: park at Bar Peraza at the pass *(degollada)*.

The Barranco de Las Lajas, the setting for this walk, is a picturesque valley with a number of reservoirs and, higher up, cascading streams and pine-wooded slopes. The hike makes a short steep descent down towards the rustic village of La Laja, followed by a short steep climb back up to the crest, from where you overlook a number of curiously-shaped volcanic chimneys — *Los Roques.*

The walk starts at the BUS STOP by the **Mirador Degollada de Peraza** (Picnic 19). Descend the signposted path at the right of the viewpoint balcony. This superbly-cobbled path leads down the hillside to La Laja (although the village is still in hiding far down to the left). Initially you overlook a valley of tumbling ridges. Just keep to the cobbled *camino* all the way down.

Crossing the first ridge, the *Roques* appear higher up in the valley: La Zarcita (left) and Ojila (right) — smooth conical volcanic chimneys. Thick, fleshy-leafed aloe plants proliferate on these barren inclines. Some 35 minutes down from the pass, charming La Laja comes into view, a small strung-out village. Ten minutes later, from the crest of a sharp ridge, you find the ideal VIEWPOINT over this peace-ful little haven (**45min**).
At this viewpoint, *leave* the main path, and follow the left fork along the steep hillside at the edge of the pine woods, passing *above* the village of **La Laja**.

Take care: the pine needles are very slippery underfoot. A bubbling stream and the green *barranco* bed below enhance the freshness of the valley floor. Five minutes later, the other path rejoins from the right. Continue above the village for another couple of minutes, then come to another fork.
The next fork, signposted 'ROQUE DE AGANDO' (**1h**), marks the beginning of your ascent: keep left here. A steep climb through pines follows. Ignore any minor paths to the left or right. The trail crosses four stream beds on wooden bridges or planks.
Higher up you reach an enchant-ing old ramshackle SHELTER with a veranda at the **Degollada del Tanque** (**1h45min**), on a crest at the edge of the wood. From here three volcanic chimneys are in view, the product of lava that solidified inside volcanic vents. The one on the left is Carmen, and the other two you identified earlier in the hike. Roque de Agando rises behind the crest to the left.

99

To make for the main road near Roque de Agando, take the path at the left of the shelter, to continue up the spine of the ridge (don't take the path behind the shelter). On the ascent, a wonderful panorama unfolds over the faded-green valleys below. Tenerife sits in the background, clearly outlined. Eventually you reach the main road just below and to the east of **Roque de Agando (2h20min)**. You will turn left on the road to continue the walk, but first follow the road (with the red/white waymarks of the **GR 131**) to the *right* for a few minutes, to a forest fire memorial and *mirador,* for a fine view down into the Barranco de Benchijigua and the route of Alternative walk 18.

From the *mirador* retrace your steps along the road. Two minutes (about 200m/yds) past the point where your path joined the road, follow the **GR 131** uphill to the left. After 10 minutes or so the trail descends to a track, which takes you down to the **Ermita de las Nieves (2h40min)**. Picnic facilities and barbecue sites have been set up here, to take advantage of the magnificent panorama.

From the chapel follow the lane downhill. After 10 minutes, 50m/yds before the lane turns sharp right downhill to the main road, head left uphill on a track (still the **GR 131**). Another track joins from the right and you pass two masts. Don't miss the magnificent views down into the Barranco de Las Lajas from the edge of the escarpment here, but be careful if it's windy! When the track fizzles out after 10 minutes, continue on the cobbled trail, which almost at once begins to drop steeply down to the main road below, 100m/yds west of the **Mirador Degollada de Peraza (3h10min)** and your BUS STOP.

The old shelter at the Degollada del Tanque, dwarfed by Roque de Ojila (top); farmer irrigating his plots in the Barranco de las Lajas (middle); the trail from La Laja up to Roque de Agando (bottom)

Walk 20: DEGOLLADA DE PERAZA • SEIMA • CASAS DE CONTRERA • DEGOLLADA DE PERAZA

See map pages 96-97; see also photograph page 104 (lower)
Distance: 14.5km/9mi; 4h40min
Grade: moderate-strenuous, with a descent/ascent of 550m/ 1800ft. You must be sure-footed and have a head for heights. Don't attempt in wet or windy weather. All on signposted paths.
Equipment: walking boots, walking stick(s), sunhat, fleece, raingear, picnic, plenty of water
Access: 🚐 to/from the Degollada de Peraza (Timetables 11,

13, 17); journey time from San Sebastián 20min, from Playa de Santiago 1h. Or 🚗: park south of the Degollada de Peraza, on the old road (now a lay-by) east of Jerduñe; deduct 30min from total times. *NB:* 🚐 lines 3 and 7 (Timetables 13, 17) stop here.
Alternative walk: Degollada de Peraza to Playa de Santiago (13km/8mi; 4h25min). Access as main walk. Follow the main walk to **Seima**, then pick up Walk 21. Almost all downhill — about 1000m/3300ft.

E levated grassy valleys and abandoned derelict farming settlements are the hallmark of this hike, and right from the outset the dramatic approach above canyon-sized valleys puts you into a hiking mood.

The walk starts at the **Degollada de Peraza**. Walk downhill along the Santiago road (the CARRETERA DEL SUR; GM3). After 15 minutes head left on a signposted track (the old road, now a lay-by, and where you join the walk if you come by car). Leave the old road in the hairpin bend: take the path that heads towards the right-hand side of the ridge. The village set on the prickly pear-covered slopes over to your right is Jerduñe. Rounding the side of the ridge, you arrive at a sheltered col, to discover the couple of buildings of **Berruga**. Keeping to the left of the buildings, the path then returns to the west side of the ridge, where a view unfolds down into the **Barranco de los Castredores**. The wide but somewhat vertiginous path descends along the base of the craggy crest, the **Alto de Tacalcuse**.
After a short climb onto a ridge, the Playa de Santiago's Hotel Tecina and golf course come

into view. Soon you'll spot an interesting outpost above you, built into and around the Tacalcuse rock face. You pass below these abandoned buildings. A good five minutes later, on coming to a signposted junction (**1h05min**), turn left for 'SEIMA'. (Later in the walk you'll return to this junction from Casas de Contrera off to the right.)
Gentle grassy slopes littered with stone walls roll away ahead of you now, and El Teide stands out clearly on the horizon over to the left. Soon you arrive at the edge of the strikingly severe **Barranco Juan de Vera**. A few minutes later you overlook Seima, its abandoned stone dwellings scattered over a hillside of rocks and grass not far below.
After less than 10 minutes' descent, you're looking down on a derelict building with a sprawling brilliant-green pepper tree in front of it. Pass to the left of the building and to the right

At 1h05min you pass below the abandoned buildings of Tacalcuse.

of the next one. During the next 10 minutes, go left at a fork and, on entering the centre of **Seima** (**1h45min**), turn right at a second, signposted fork. Now use the notes for Walk 21 from the 4h05min-point (page 105) as far as **Casas de Contrera** (**2h30min**), shown on page 104.

To return to the Degollada de Peraza, take the signposted path that ascends to the left of the main two-storied house. *(The Alternative walk descends left here, to Playa de Santiago.)* Climb the rocky crest behind the house. After about 15 minutes, you pass to the right of a derelict stone building, with a wheat threshing floor just below. High gentle slopes keep appearing, revealing the remains of an amazingly-large area of cultivation in days gone by.

A little over 10 minutes above the last building, some more buildings appear at the right of the path. A couple of minutes further uphill, the way passes over bedrock. Continue straight uphill, and ignore the minor path going off to the right. After the remains of a low wall appear to the right of the path, the way is again clearly defined.

Back at the SEIMA JUNCTION (**3h15min**), turn left to rejoin your outgoing path, after two minutes passing by the houses at Tacalcuse.

From the pass at **Berruga** continue up the GM3 and when you reach the GM2 (**4h25min**), turn right and continue to the BAR PERAZA (**4h40min**), just to the right of the *mirador*. Flag your bus down opposite the bar.

Walk 21: SAN SEBASTIAN • PLAYA DE LA GUANCHA • EL CABRITO • PLAYA DE SANTIAGO

Map begins on pages 108-109, ends on pages 96-97
Distance: 19km/12mi; 7h
Grade: very strenuous and long, with ascents/descents of 1100m/3600ft overall, on stony paths. You must be sure-footed and have a head for heights on the climb over to El Cabrito. A walk for the very fit! Red/white way-marking throughout (GR 132). *Note that there is no shade!*
Equipment: walking boots, walking stick(s), sunhat, fleece, raingear, swimwear, picnic, plenty of water

Access: 🚌 (Timetables 11, 12, 13, 17) or ⛴ (Timetable 18) to San Sebastián
To return: 🚌 (Timetable 13) or ⛴ (Timetable 18) from Playa de Santiago
Shorter walk: San Sebastián — Playa de la Guancha — San Sebastián (10km/6.2mi; 3h20min). Moderate, with ascents/descents of 400m/1300ft overall; access and equipment as above. Follow the main walk to **Playa de la Guancha** (**1h25min**) and return the same way.

Up at the crack of dawn, you'll catch the sun rising over the *cumbre* and perhaps see the morning ferry sailing across to Tenerife. Then, struggling in and out of *barrancos*, you'll cross a barren landscape strewn with rock, where ravines narrow into shady fissures. At the mouth of one of these sits the tiny outpost of El Cabrito — an oasis of greenery accessible only by boat or on foot.

Setting out from **San Sebastián**, follow the beach promenade southwest. Pass the FOOTBALL GROUND, then turn right and take the river bed road/track to ENDESA (the town power plant). Just past the plant entrance, go left on the sign-posted path running alongside the grounds (red/white way-marks of the **GR 132**). After a few minutes' uphill, the remains of an old cobbled path come underfoot.

A 20-minute climb brings you to the crest of a ridge. The path then passes above a WOODEN CROSS (which topples over from time to time), from where there is a fine view back to the capital. On the slopes high above stands the great Sacred Heart monument. You cross the **Barranco del Revolcadero** (**40min**) and, still ascending, cross the faint remains of a dirt track. Thirty

minutes later you cross another ridge (**1h10min**) and catch sight of Playa del Cabrito, set deep in the sheer coastline ahead, and Playa de la Guancha directly below, a lonely beach set in a forbidding landscape of dark jagged cliffs rising from an aquamarine sea. The path twists down into a side-ravine and through a dry, boulder-strewn stream bed, where lime-green *balo* floods the *barranco* floor. You pass a cottage and some shacks behind **Playa de la Guancha** (**1h25min**). This is a good place to swim, but *take care:* the beach shelves steeply.

From here the route continues past the cottage and shacks up the right-hand side of the **Barranco de la Guancha**. Some 20 minutes from the beach, the way swings left across the *barranco* (**1h45min**) and climbs

103

Playa del Cabrito and (left) the abandoned Casas de Contrera

the far side. Fifteen minutes up, the path suddenly turns left, up stone steps. (Ignore the faint trail to the right here — it was originally a variation of the GR, but it is not maintained by the *cabildo*.)

On reaching a CREST (**2h10min**), an exhilarating sight greets you: you look straight down into a deep *barranco,* where knurls (knobby ridges resembling steep stairways) tumble down the sides. To the left you spot the corner of a tiny Garden of Eden — El Cabrito. The full beauty of this verdant outpost is revealed a little further on, when you look down on its tapestry of banana groves, fruit trees and vegetable plots. To reach it, head up left, then cross over to the right-hand side of this sheer ridge, where a steep, gravelly path drops you in

zigzags down into the **Barranco Juan de Vera**. The **El Cabrito** *finca* (formerly a croft, now a holiday resort) sits behind the thick stone wall that keeps the *barranco* from overflowing after heavy rain.

Cross the *barranco* and follow the wall to the left for some 100m/yds, then use the stone 'steps' to climb over the wall and turn left along a track to the long stony **Playa del Cabrito** (**2h35min**). Continue along the shore and, nearer the quay, follow the track to the right, into a plantation. By a row of houses, pick up your ongoing cobbled trail to the left. (When the way forks above some plots, turn sharp left.)

The well-cobbled trail takes you huffing and puffing up to a FLAT-TOPPED CREST (**3h15min**). Follow the crest inland and scramble over a dyke. Higher up, you briefly enter a water-course and leave it on a faint trail that curves to the left. At a junction just below the crest (the other end of the faint, neglected GR variation), keep left.

Higher still (**4h**), you catch a glimpse of the Hotel Tecina and the gardens above Santiago and then the abandoned hamlet of Seima, superbly located in open countryside overlooking the sea. A little over five minutes later you pass through **Seima** (**4h05min**). Have a look at the well-preserved old oven *(horno)* just below the first cluster of buildings (on your right). Then pass through a row of abandoned houses until you reach a junction, where there is another old *horno* behind a stone wall on the right. (*Walk 20 joins at this junction.*)

Turn left here and (now referring to the map on pages 96-97) follow the clear trail around the valley. Once in a while you will spot the faded red/white flashes of the **GR 132**. After clambering over a natural wall of broken rock, you see Casas de Contrera, an old farmstead two *barrancos* away. Past the first *barranco* (**Barranco de Guincho**), keep right at a fork. The trail fades as you approach the second stream bed, **Barranco de Contrera**: just continue up the valley floor for about 50m/yds, following the faint waymarks and cairns.

On reaching the abandoned **Casas de Contrera** (**4h50min**), you'll probably want to explore the main building — the grand two-storied house shown opposite. Some interesting artefacts are lying about, but take care; the masonry may be weak. The trail forks below this house (SIGNPOST): your onward route goes down to the left. (*But for Walk 20, take the trail ascending to the left of the house.*)

After five minutes, cross a dry stream bed. Re-crossing almost at once, keep to the main trail, passing below farm buildings. A good 10 minutes from Contrera, ignore a path ascending to the

left. Then pick up the main stream again (**Barranco de la Vasa**): cross it and pass three stone houses in succession (**5h10min**).

The trail descends beside and then in a tiny *barranco*. After crossing the *barranco*, it passes to the right of a stone building and then bends right. Ten minutes later you reach the edge of the *barranco*. From here the route descends steadily into the meagre banana groves of the **Barranco de Chinguarime**, where you cross the river bed and join a track (**5h50min**).

Follow the track south just a short way, then pick up the trail on the right. Below the lowest house at **Casas del Joradillo** the old *camino* meets a road, but just past the houses you can pick up your trail again to descend into the next *barranco*. Rejoining the road, follow it almost to its highest point, then cut back right on the trail (next to a SMALL CONCRETE BUILDING). Cross the crest and descend into another *barranco*. Cross the road once more, and continue down the path. You cross yet another *barranco* and join a road at a Y-fork. Follow the road south, uphill, ignoring the road left to Playa de Tapahuga.

Now follow the road between the hotel Jardín Tecina and the golf course to the BUS STOP in **Playa de Santiago** — on the main road, 50m/yds to the left (**7h**).

Walk 22: CAMINO FORESTAL DE MAJONA TO SAN SEBASTIAN

Distance: 9.2km/5.5mi; 2h45min

Grade: Easy-moderate, with overall ascents of about 300m/1000ft. You must be sure-footed and have a head for heights. Don't attempt on wet or windy days: danger of rockfall.

Equipment: walking boots, sunhat, fleece, windproof, long trousers, raingear, picnic, water, dog deterrent (stick, stone, Dog Dazer)

Access: 🚐 (Timetable 12) to the Camino Forestal de Majona (Majona mountain road); journey time from San Sebastián 15min. The bus stop, called 'Las Casetas', is just before the Mirador A Lazcano. *Note:* the Camino Forestal de Majona is a very narrow and dangerous road, not recommended for motorists — it's too narrow for two cars to pass, there is no fencing and danger of rockfall.

To return: 🚐 (Timetables 11, 12, 13, 17) from San Sebastián

Alternative walk: Cuevas Blancas (12.2km/7.5mi; 3h 05min). *The rock strata to be seen on this variation are among the island's most interesting geological features. Easy-moderate if you use our suggested route*, with overall ascents/descents of about 400m/1300ft. You must be sure-footed and have a good sense of direction: at times you will have to make your way over rocky terrain without a path, but it is quite straightforward *in clear weather*. (Don't attempt this walk in poor visibility or on wet or windy days.) Equipment and access as above. Or by 🚗: park at the side of the GM1 by the Majona mountain road (at the KM8 road marker, about 300m before the first tunnel, when coming from San Sebastián); be

sure not to block the entrance to the road! Follow the main walk up to the pass of **La Gerode**. A minute later, you *could* turn left on the 'official' (presumably well maintained) path signposted to 'CUEVAS BLANCAS', we *do not recommend it: it is very narrow, vertiginous and dangerous*. It's far easier and safer to follow the main walk to the 55MIN-POINT and then fork left around the hillside, heading back the way you came, but now well above the (hardly visible) Casas de Jaragán. Ahead you will see a GULLY WITH PALMS: descend to this gully, where you will meet the 'official' route (north of the point where it is dangerous). Follow it to the right, crossing an old THRESHING FLOOR. Coming to a fork, keep to the left side of the ROCKY OUTCROP (on the return, you will rejoin your path from the right-hand fork). A little over 10 minutes later, surrounded by goats, and with dogs going berserk, you arrive at **Casas de Cuevas Blancas** (**1h25min**). *Make sure the dogs are tied up before venturing too close* — and give the *casas* a wide berth: pass below them. From here you'll see your ongoing path across the valley on your right. A rough animals' trail will take you past the 'white caves' (**Cuevas Blancas**) and onto this path. Some 15 minutes from the homestead, as the path vanishes on a crest, follow cairns up to the ridge. Several minutes up, the way levels out, and about seven minutes later you're back on your outgoing path: follow it to the left and retrace your outgoing route back to the **Camino Forestal de Majona** and the LAS CASETAS BUS STOP (**3h05min**).

This walk is best begun early in the morning, to appreciate the spectacular play of light and shade on the *cumbre* (see photograph above). The Alternative walk is perhaps even better, with fascinating geological strata, herds of goats and small flocks of sheep roaming grassy slopes — and hidden corners with isolated stands of palms or rocks dripping with lichen.

Start out at the 'LAS CASETAS' BUS STOP at the junction of the **GM1 (Carretera del Norte)** and the **Camino Forestal de Majona,** where you leave your transport. Follow the mountain road *(camino forestal)* uphill. You pass a path off left after 80m/yds — Walk 23 descends it. Now heading east, already you can look down over the **Barranco de Agua Jilva,** on its way to San Sebastián. And behind you lies the *cumbre,* a backbone of forested ridges radiating seaward. The narrow mountain road leads to the pass of **La Gerode (35min),** from where you can look down into the enormous Barranco de las Casas, slicing into the massif.

From the pass take the signposted fork to the right, and at a junction a minute further uphill *keep right again* (the route to the left, the officially signposted path to 'Cuevas Blancas', is *narrow, vertiginous and **dangerous**).* Your

Looking west to Los Roques from the Camino Forestal de Majona (top of the page) and (above) the Cuevas Blancas: built into white tuff, they are now used as storerooms.

trail to San Sebastián, beside a WATER PIPE, makes its way across the rocky hillside and climbs the nose of the ridge, sometimes over bedrock. Five minutes along, you reach a craggy outcrop below a cave. The path sidles up against the sheer face of the ridge, which slides down into the *barranco.* Ten minutes further along, bits of rubbish, broken glass, and dogs barking, alert you to the **Casas de Jaragán** (**50min**), a homestead high in the rock above. Continue straight ahead — beside a white- and pink-hued 'sandwich' in the rock face. You quickly reach another crest (**55min**). (*The Alternative walk turns left here on no particular path, just rounding the contours of the hillside.*) Walk ahead to a SIGNPOST indicating San Sebastián and turn left, keeping an eye open for cairns and paint marks. After some 100m/yds along this path, when you come to a waymarked rock, turn sharp right downhill. Small cairns will keep you on the trail.

You descend a winding (and potentially ankle-twisting) path into a side-ravine. Some 20 minutes down from the crest, when a path joins from the left, keep straight on (the right-hand fork). Cross a DYKE and later enter the **Barranco del Rincón**, a narrow dry ravine lined from top to bottom with crumbled stone walls. Circle the *barranco*, ignoring a path heading back left towards Aluce, and soon pass a couple of TELEVISION AERIALS set in the rock (**1h55min**).

You eventually join a road; cross over to another road and pick up your path a few metres/yards to the right. Rejoin the road, and follow it straight ahead over a roundabout and then past houses. A good 10 minutes later, watch for steps descending to the right, off an alley (CALLE NUÑEZ DE BALBOA) running parallel with the street you are on (by a supermarket on the right). Follow this stairway, ignoring crossing streets, all the way down into **San Sebastián**, where you will emerge at the church, **Nuestra Señora de la Asunción** (**2h45min**).

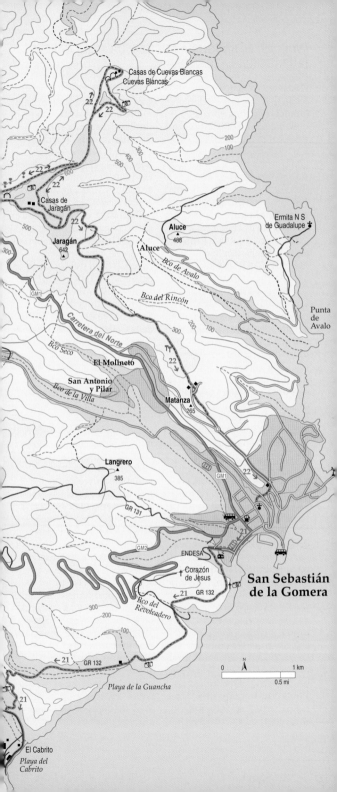

Walk 23: HERMIGUA • ENCHEREDA • LAS CASETAS (MIRADOR A LAZCANO)

Distance: 16.5km/10.5mi; 5h50min

Grade: strenuous, with an overall ascent of 650/2100ft and a descent of 200m/650ft to the Las Casetas bus stop on the GM1

Equipment: walking boots, walking stick(s), sunhat, fleece, windproof, long trousers, raingear, picnic, plenty of water

Access: 🚌 to Hermigua (Timetable 12); journey time from San Sebastián 35min. Alight at the DISA petrol station north of the church.

To return: 🚌 from the 'Las Casetas' bus stop on the GM1 (Timetable 12); journey time 15min. If you are returning to San Sebastián, be ready to signal to the driver as the bus shoots round the corner.

Short walk: Playa de la Caleta — Punta San Lorenzo — Playa de la Caleta (5.3km/3.3mi; 2h). Easy-moderate, with overall ascents/descents of 300m/1000ft; equipment as main walk, plus swimwear. Access: 🚗 to/from Playa de la Caleta (Picnic 23); park above the beach. Or 🚌 as main walk, then on foot to Playa de la Caleta, and back (adds 1h each way). A little gem of a coastal walk, suitable for all ages, on a wide, well-protected path. Follow the *Alternative walk* opposite from **Playa de la Caleta** to the 1h50min-point in that walk and turn left. The path reaches a viewpoint on a crest and then turns into a short side-*barranco*. Cross the stream bed and climb out the other side, to be met by more stunning views of the wild coastline. When you reach the end of the path at **Punta San Lorenzo** (**1h**), some rickety steps lead down to a small pool and a pebbly beach.

Only swim here when the sea is dead calm! Return the same way to **Playa de la Caleta** with its small bar/restaurant (**2h**).

Alternative walk: Hermigua — Playa de la Caleta — El Palmar — (Taguluche) — Hermigua (13km/8mi; 4h15min). Moderate, with overall ascents/descents of 550m/1800ft and a 15-minute stretch of path demanding a head for heights. Equipment as main walk, plus swimwear. Access as main walk or by 🚗: park near the DISA petrol station. Follow the main walk to the 40min-point, then keep ahead on the lane down to **Playa de la Caleta** (Picnic 23). Swimming is safe here when the sea is calm. Ten minutes back up the lane, you'll see a renovated farm building with well-tended vineyards on the far side of the *barranco*. About 80m/yds further up the lane, turn left on a path with a large walkers' SIGNBOARD, into the lushly-cultivated valley floor. Cross the stream bed (**Barranco de Montoro**), climb into some terraced plots and turn left immediately. Ignore a fork off to the right and round the hillside. At a fork where a path goes left to Punta San Lorenzo (**1h50min**), turn right. Ten minutes later you round a nose of hillside and descend across a palm-filled stream bed, the **Barranco Cañada Barraca**. Several minutes up a rocky ridge on the far side, fork left at a junction. When you join a track near the farmstead of **El Palmar** (**2h10min**), yappy dogs will appear. *(From here you could take a straightforward detour to Taguluche — allow an extra hour: just follow the track from El Palmar and, when you reach the main* *track, keep left for Taguluche. Returning, keep straight along the main track — the left fork.)* To make for Hermigua however, continue up the track alongside the farmstead, then leave it almost immediately past a stone and tile-roofed building, ascending a path to the right (just in front of a big rock with white lettering: 'PALMAR'). A few minutes uphill you rejoin the main track just past an isolated farmstead and below a house. Turning right, follow it all the way back to **Hermigua**, 2 hours away (**4h15min**).

Leaving the lush green banana plantations behind, you ascend the severe walls of the Barranco de Monteforte and bid farewell to Hermigua. Ahead lies one of the loneliest, bleakest corners of the island. This inhospitable landscape of razor-back ridges and sheer ravines may not appeal to everyone. But for those who find beauty in desolate landscapes, there are heather-capped crests and a rainbow of volcanic hues in the rock to brighten the way.

Setting out from the DISA PETROL STATION in **Hermigua**, follow the main road south towards San Sebastián for about 25m/yds. Then descend the first flight of steps on the left, dropping into the banana groves. Cross the **Barranco de Monteforte** on a footbridge and then keep right when you come onto a wide lane. At the end of the lane climb up left to the road and turn right. Three minutes along, fork left uphill on a road (signposted 'PLAYA CALETA, EL PALMAR'). Just 100m/yds further on, at a junction, go straight ahead, now on a lane. From here there's a good view over Hermigua's banana plots and beach.

Crossing the **Camiña** ridge (**40min**), turn sharp right at the junction, now on a track. *(But for the Alternative walk, keep straight ahead on the tarred lane for Playa de la Caleta.)* An impenetrable wall of mountains crosses the landscape in front of you and tumbles off into the sea. Ascending gradually into the hills, you find them surprisingly green and grassy. Trees begin appearing: short bushy pines, palms and, soon, junipers. The track contours, curling in and out of the hillsides. Ignore all turn-offs to the left (some signposted to La Caleta, El Palmar, others chained off and private. Stay on the main track with the WATER PIPE.

Eventually you begin climbing the **Riscos de Juel** (**2h**) in a series of tight zigzags. You pass through old vineyards and come into a colony of palms. Rock walls dripping with vegetation rise sharply above you. Having climbed high up the face of the escarpment, the banana plantations of Hermigua come into view once more. The track is very damaged from several years' of heavy rainfall and often is little more than a path. You pass a couple of STONE FARM SHEDS (**2h35min**) clinging to the hillside. On cloudless days, the view across the tumbling naked ridges and out over the rocky shoreline onto a white-capped sea is superb. Further up, off a sharp bend, you can look down into the plunging **Barranco de Taguluche** — a valley full of vineyards, its vertical walls speckled with bright green

The lone homestead of Enchereda almost blends in with the browns of the surrounding hills, but its bright green terraced gardens give it away.

houseleeks. Reaching the tree-line, you come into pine forest with a touch of laurel in its midst. Most unexpectedly, a short stretch of concrete and stone paving comes under foot. Crossing over the *cumbre,* you'll more than likely get blasted by the wind.

Continuing deeper into this wilderness, you drop down into the **Barranco de Juel**. Cloaks of heather slip down off the shoulders of the crests. Flocks graze the lower grassy slopes, and you'll bump into healthy cows and calves dawdling along the track (please pass them quietly). Later, when you enter another valley (**Barranco de Galion**), neglected plots and the remains of stone walls tell the story of homesteads abandoned. The only sounds you'll hear are the shrill calls of the kestrel and the wing-beating of fleeing quail.

Eventually you head into yet another valley, the **Barranco de las Casas**. The lone homestead of **Enchereda** (**4h45min**) comes into sight, almost blending in with the browns of the denuded hills. The goats are milked here at midday; the best cheese on the island reputedly comes from these hills and valleys. Along here the eroded hillsides are a feast of colour: maroon, russet, faded gold, rusty orange.

Ten minutes beyond the homestead, leave the track by climbing steps up to the right one minute after passing a small electricity substation.

A steady climb takes you up through ferns and rock-roses. You look out right over the enormous Barranco de las Casas. Twenty minutes up, above a pine grove, you come to a path junction on a col. Turn right here and descend to the GM1 at the LAS CASETAS BUS STOP just east of the **Mirador A Lazcano** (**5h50min**) — where the Camino Forestal de Majona joins the road (for the San Sebastián bus, stand well away from the bend).

114

Walk 24: HERMIGUA • EL CEDRO • HERMIGUA

See map pages 112-113; see also photograph page 88
Distance: 9km/5.6mi; 4h20min
Grade: very strenuous, with an ascent of 600m/2000ft. You must be sure-footed and have a head for heights. Don't attempt in wet or windy weather. *Note:* these hills are often covered in cloud. Most of the route follows signposted trails.
Equipment: walking boots, walking stick(s), sunhat, fleece, windproof, gloves, long trousers, raingear, picnic, water
Access: 🚌 to El Convento, one of the upper districts *(barrios)* in Hermigua (Timetable 12); journey time from San Sebastián 30min. Alight at the bus stop near the plaza and the church. Or 🚗: park about 50m/yds north of this plaza, at a large car park on the left.
To return: 🚌 from Hermigua (Timetable 12); journey time to San Sebastián 35min. If you parked at El Convento, you *could* take the bus back to your car (it's only 650m further south, but the 100m ascent on the main road is tiring in the afternoon heat).

Following a watercourse, you head into the depths of the Monteforte and Cedro *barrancos,* where sheer-sided walls, lavishly draped in vegetation, tower above you. Scaling these walls, and passing the islands highest and largest waterfall, you stumble upon a sprinkling of cottages at El Cedro, set at the edge of the laurel forest. Homeward bound, a tranquil forestry track lures you down a wooded crest … to your steep and rocky descent path, from where you'll have a superb panorama over the Hermigua valley. The circuit makes an ideal day out for motorists just itching to pull on their boots.

Start out on the main road at El Convento. Cross the road from the bus stop near the plaza and the church and pick up the signposted path to 'EL CEDRO' 10m/yds to the left: wide steps that take you steeply up to a road in the *barrio* of San Pedro (5min). Turn right up this road, heading below Roque de San Pedro, growing straight up out of the *barranco* wall. (There are in fact *two* rocks here, and they are often called 'Los Gemelos' — The Twins.)
In about 10 minutes the trail takes you left, off the road and over a bridge, to walk along the left-hand side of the Barranco de Monteforte. Ignore two sets of steps on your left and in just a few minutes you re-cross to the

Signposting on Walk 23. Signposted walks should be maintained by the island government and the routes highlighted on the Cabildo map recommended on page 36.

right-hand side. Now, immersed in banana plantations and garden plots, the straightforward route heads up the valley, for much of

115

the time in the company of a WATER PIPE.

Ascending stone-paved steps, the path eventually crosses to the left-hand side of the *barranco* and climbs above a large WATER TANK. The way narrows to no more than a passage, and soon you can see the end — a half-moon cliff-face with a fine veil of water trickling over it. Steps take you up and around the right-

hand side of a DAM WALL (**Embalse de los Tiles; 1h**). Continue on the trail 100m/yds past the dam, zigzagging up the right-hand wall of the *barranco* to a pass. This ascent is awesome — affording the wonderful view back down over the Hermigua valley and the Roque San Pedro shown on the cover, as well as to the **Salto de Água**, the highest waterfall on the island.

The terraces of Monteforte

El Cedro (Walks 15 and 24). Short walk 15-1 is the best way to see this charming little community, if you don't have the time or stamina for a long hike.

An ELECTRICITY PYLON marks the PASS at the top of the valley (**1h45min**), from where you look straight onto **El Cedro**, a handful of houses set in an untidy cultivated basin, embraced by the laurel forest. Following the stream bed, you arrive at a CAMPING AREA and the popular BAR/RESTAURANT LA VISTA just above it.

From the car park above LA VISTA, follow the steep road climbing to the right. At a junction, pick up a wide path ascending the bank on the right (above a greyish-coloured house, the CASA RURAL EL REFUGIO). A minute later, pick up another path on the right. Still climbing, you enter a cool dense forest, steeped in moss and lichen. On meeting a FORESTRY TRACK (**2h30min**), turn right downhill. After about 35 minutes of descent, turn sharp right on another track. But just 35m/yds after turning off, take a signposted path down to the left.

Your descent to Hermigua has begun. You head down the neck of a ridge and rejoin the track. A minute later, the track fizzles out into a path, perhaps a bit overgrown. Rounding a ridge, you look straight down the valley as it opens out to the sea. Soon you join an old cobbled trail. Pass to the right of a derelict FARM BUILDING (**3h25min**), magnificently perched overlooking the valley. Step down through abandoned terraces. Crossing a *barranco*, keep straight on round the hillside and pass below a WATER TANK on the top of the ridge. When you come to the **Ermita de San Juan** (**3h55min**), take time to soak up another superb view down the valley.

Coming back from the chapel, you *could* follow the lane ahead back to El Convento, allowing an hour; see map. But the main walk keeps to the trail: descend the steps to the left just at the end of the lane. A little over 10 minutes below the chapel, pass some houses and join a road. Cross it, walk along to the left for a few metres/yards, then descend steps. At the next road crossing, your continuing steps are a few metres/yards to the right. Squeeze past rustic cottages and down to the MAIN ROAD (**4h20min**) in **Hermigua** by the ETHNOGRAPHIC MUSEUM (BUS STOP). If you've left a car at El Convento, walk up the main road to fetch it — about 650m/ half a mile, with an extra 100m/ 330ft of ascent... or take the bus.

Walk 25: AGULO • CENTRO DE VISITANTES JUEGO DE BOLAS • EMBALSE DE AMALAHUIGUE • EL TION • VALLEHERMOSO

Note: The Garajonay Park Visitors' Centre (Juego de Bolas) is open daily from 09.30-16.30.

Distance: 12km/7.5mi; 4h25min

Grade: fairly strenuous, with ascents/descents of 600m/2000ft overall. Beyond El Tión, the descent is steep and gravelly; you must be sure-footed and have a head for heights. Don't attempt in wet or windy weather.

Equipment: walking boots, walking stick(s), sunhat, fleece, wind/rainproofs, long trousers, picnic, water

Access: 🚌 to Agulo (Timetable 12); journey time from San Sebastián 50min. Or 🚗: car park off the GM1 just outside Agulo

To return: 🚌 from Vallehermoso (Timetable 12); journey time to San Sebastián 1h25min, or to Agulo for your car 35min

Short walks

1 Mirador de Abrante (3.5km/ 2mi; 55min). Fairly easy, with a descent/ascent of 100m/330ft. Equipment as above (less long trousers and stick). Access by 🚗: park at the Centro de Visitantes (Car tour 6). Use notes from the 2h-point in the *Alternative walk* to reach the *mirador*, then return the same way.

2 Agulo — Embalse de Amalahuigue — Las Rosas (7km/ 4.5mi; 2h30min). Fairly strenuous, with an overall ascent of 600m/2000ft. Equipment and access as main walk. Follow the main walk to the 2h15min-point, then cross the road and go straight down a lane through Las Rosas and on to the main road. The bus stop (Vallehermoso 🚌, as above) is at the junction.

3 Las Rosas — Embalse de Amalahuigue — Vallehermoso (7km/4.5mi; 1h50min). Easy, except for the short but steep

descent of about 100m/330ft beyond El Tión. You must be sure-footed and have a head for heights, and don't attempt in wet or windy weather. Equipment as main walk. Access: 🚌 to Las Rosas (Vallehermoso bus, Timetable 12); the stop is just past the turn-off to La Palmita. Follow the lane from the bus stop straight up to the reservoir. Follow the main walk from the 2h15min-point to the end. Return as for the main walk.

Alternative walk: Agulo — La Palmita — Juego de Bolas — Mirador de Abrante — Agulo (12km/7.5mi; 4h05min). Grade and equipment as main walk. Access: 🚌 to/from Agulo (Timetable 12), or 🚗: park off the main road at the edge of the village. From the BUS STOP in **Agulo** follow the MAIN ROAD TOWARDS VALLEHERMOSO, past the POST OFFICE. A minute along, just past the PHARMACY, climb signposted stone steps up through terracing. Cross a lane and, a minute later, the main road. The trail heads steeply up towards the base of the cliffs and the, without respite, climbs in zigzags to a pass at the **Mirador de Agulo** (**45min**). The route swings right, away from the stream, to ascend above the **Embalse de Agulo**. On reaching a tarred lane, follow it up the valley; two minutes later, just above a holiday complex, turn left on a road which later becomes a track. Fifteen minute from the dam, the track crosses to the left-hand side of the stream; five minutes later ignore a short-cut to the Visitors' Centre (via a bridge on the right). From here the way is tarred, then stone-laid. Two

Picnic 25a overlooks Agulo, the most superbly-sited village on the island. This photo was taken just below the Mirador de Agulo (Alternative walk).

minutes later, cross a small ravine, then take the *second* of two paths climbing the hillside to the right. At a junction three minutes up, turn right and climb to the **San Isidro** chapel and PICNIC SITE at **La Palmita** (**1h40min**). Now ascend to the Aceviños/El Cedro road, and turn right to the **Juego de Bolas** (Garajonay Visitors' Centre; **2h**). Leaving, take the road between the centre and BAR/ RESTAURANT TAMBOR (red/white waymarked **GR 132**). After 100m/yds, continue straight ahead on a washed-out red earthen track. About 15 minutes from the Visitors' Centre, past a small pine wood, turn half left up a minor track. Your sign-posted turn-off to Agulo lies a minute along, on the left. But first, continue straight ahead down the crest for less than 10 minutes, to the **Mirador de Abrante** (**2h25min**). This is a new visitors' centre/bar with a spectacular glass skywalk over the enormous drop above Agulo. However, it has never been

opened and as we went to press had no proper access road. Back at the turn-off for Agulo, turn right; the path follows a greyish erosion gully. Soon you're on a cobbled trail, with fine views over the Barranco de Las Rosas. When the trail forks above a CHARMING OLD HOUSE, turn right with the **GR 132**. Meeting the main road, follow it to the right for 50m/yds, then turn left back onto the trail. Rounding a nose of rock, you descend to the village CEMETERY, from where a cobbled road leads back to the centre of **Agulo** (**4h05min**).

Y ou'll remember this walk for its enchanting valleys. The first, finely etched into the landscape, leaves a deep impression — both figuratively and literally. You climb into scrub-daubed hills, dotted with dwellings. Approaching the tree-line, settlement thins and, from the top of a crest, you overlook an immense cauldron of cascading ridges. In their midst sits Vallehermoso. A most rewarding descent follows, as you drop into a plunging valley drenched with palms, its high rock walls flecked with pines. Here the terraced plots are a work of art; you have the feeling you could stroll in this valley forever.

Off the bus in **Agulo**, **start off** by heading up the ROAD TOWARDS VALLEHERMOSO, then take the first right turn into a cobbled street. Follow this straight through Agulo, ignoring all side-streets. At a T-junction, turn right, passing the village square with its domed CHURCH and old houses with high latticed windows. Keep the church on your right and continue on a cobbled lane, ignoring turn-offs. You can see the cemetery in the distance. Banana groves sever the three separate *barrios* (districts) that make up the village. Some 25m/yds beyond the cemetery, climb a wide cobbled trail half-left up the hillside (red/white waymarked **GR 132**). Tenerife sits just across the sea, a vista of which Agulo is justly proud (Picnic 25a). On reaching the VALLEHERMOSO ROAD again (**20min**), turn right and walk about 50m/yds uphill, to find your continuing trail on the left. You head steeply uphill on cobbles (ignore the minor branch-off to the left).

At a junction about 35 minutes from the road, just beyond a CHARMING OLD HOUSE with verandas, your trail (still the **GR 132**) turns abruptly up to the left towards the JUEGO DE BOLAS. Mounting the crest of the ridge, the path follows a deeply-eroded watercourse and crosses a ridge soaked in rich volcanic hues. (*Note:* 10 minutes down the crest of this ridge is the sign-posted Mirador de Abrante overlooking Agulo. The time for this detour has *not* been included in the main walk.) Follow the **GR 132** past the turn-off to the

mirador, to a wide path/track just *over* the crest. Turn right uphill here. A sweeping view up the Barranco de Agulo follows. Joining a road, you come to the **Centro de Visitantes Juego de Bolas** (**1h35min**). There's a fine garden with native plants, handicraft displays, and an informative film devoted to the Garajonay National Park.

Revived, set off up the adjoining LAGUNA GRANDE ROAD. A few minutes beyond the turn-off to La Palmita and Aceviños (and after ignoring a first path to the right), turn right downhill with the **GR 132** on a trail behind a chain barrier. A minute along, cross a road and continue down into a tributary valley of the Las Rosas *barranco*. The slightly overgrown trail passes to the right of a chained off private property, crosses a stream bed and climbs straight up the other side. It runs between a couple of houses, crosses the end of a track and then rises alongside an enclosed, abandoned vineyard on the left. After five minutes' ascent, on the top of the crest, the path reaches some buildings (almost hidden by vegetation). Just before the buildings, keep right on a path alongside a small WATER PIPE. Continuing to the right, you emerge on another crest and pass above two POWER PYLONS. This is the edge of the

heather belt bordering the laurel forest.

The trail continues left round the hillside, passes another PYLON on the next crest and drops down over the crest. Joining another path, turn right, descending steeply to an access road. Follow this downhill; then, just past the last house on the crest, descend concrete steps on the left to another road and the **Amalahuigue Reservoir** (2h15min). *(Short walk 2 heads down to Las Rosas here, and Short walk 3 joins here.)*

Crossing the reservoir wall, you look down into Las Rosas. At the end of the wall, go left on the road, ignoring several side-roads and tracks. As you circle the top of the valley, a road and then a track (the **GR 132**) join from the right. Keeping to the road, after about 250m/yds you reach a *mirador* at **Rosa de las**

Piedras (2h55min; Picnic 25b), with a view across an immense cauldron filled with cascading ridges and glowing green vegetable plots. Next to it is the friendly restaurant Roque Blanco with great views as well as good food — a pleasant place for a refreshment break. Follow

Descending through El Tión

the road past the *mirador*, ignoring three roads to the left. The road heads right and descends into the valley, hugging the sheer hillside. Ignore all side roads as you wind downhill. At the end of the road, barely 15 minutes down, descend a few steep steps and continuing on a narrow path. You drop down to terraces and cut across them to the stone houses of **El Tión**, balancing on a narrow ridge high in the valley. You meet a fork here: keep right on the steep gravelly path straight down this sheer-sided ridge (inexpe-

rienced walkers may find the first few minutes unnerving). You have a good view of **Roque El Cano**, a landmark for all walks around Vallehermoso. On meeting a TRACK (**3h40min**), follow it downhill into the setting shown below. Around 35 minutes down (five minutes after the way becomes tarred for the second time), turn left on a path. When you rejoin the road, follow it downhill to the MAIN ROAD in **Valleher-moso**. Then turn left uphill to the roundabout and BUS STOP (**4h 25min**).

Roque El Cano rises above the 'valley of 1001 palms' at Vallehermoso, the highlight of this walk.

Walk 26: VALLEHERMOSO • LA MESETA • CHORROS DE EPINA • VALLEHERMOSO

See map page 127
Distance: 13km/8mi; 4h40min
Grade: strenuous, with an ascent of 600m/2000ft at the outset. You must be sure-footed and have a head for heights. The path up to La Meseta (GR 131) is sometimes overgrown, and in places narrow, steep and slippery underfoot. Don't attempt in wet weather. The walk partly follows red/white waymarked trails (GR 131 and GR 132).
Equipment: walking boots, walking stick(s), sunhat, fleece, windproof, long trousers, long-sleeved shirt, raingear, picnic, plenty of water
Access: 🚌 to/from Vallehermoso (Timetables 12, 14, 15); journey time from San Sebastián 1h25min. Or 🚗: park in the village, in the car park by the roundabout.
Short walk: Presa de los Gallos (10.8km/6.7mi; 2h 30min return). Easy, almost level walking. Access as Picnic 26, page 11, or by 🚌 to the restaurant of Chorros de Epina, and walk down the road to the Meseta forestry track. Follow the track to where it ends at the

small reservoir *(presa)*; you skirt the laurel forest, with fine views over the impressive valleys surrounding Vallehermoso and accompanied by a host of bright flowers in spring.
Alternative walk: Las Hayas — La Meseta — Vallehermoso (13km/8mi; 4h25min). Moderate, with a descent of about 800m/2625ft; equipment as main walk. Access: 🚌 to Las Hayas (Timetables 11, 14, 16) or 🚗; return by taxi from Vallehermoso — to your base or your car. To begin, FOLLOW SHORT WALK 12-2 on page 78. From the **Jardín de las Creces** picnic area keep ahead on the forestry road (**GR 131**; signposted 'CARRETERA DORSAL 0,7KM), instead of turning off left. When you meet the main road, turn left. After 100m/yds turn right on a trail signposted to Vallehermoso. This partially-overgrown and sometimes steep path (still the red/white waymarked **GR 131**) takes you down to the CAMINO FORESTAL DE LA MESETA (**1h25min**), where you meet and follow the main walk from the 1h45min-point.

F or years the GR trail up to La Meseta has tended to be overgrown, but this is still a popular hike. The walk circles what looks like a great crater with hundreds of valleys etched into it. The La Meseta forestry track, which runs along the fringe of the laurel woods, provides a pleasant interlude in this otherwise harsh, rocky terrain.

Set out by leaving **Vallehermoso** on the road branching south off the roundabout, past the BAR AMAYA on the plaza and the POST OFFICE (Calle Triana, the **GR 131**). At the T-junction turn right. The GR 131 splits 30m/yds further on: ignore the signposted branch to the left and continue up the road into the

Barranco del Valle. You wind above banana plots and vegetable gardens. Just where the road curves sharply left (towards the Embalse de la Encantadora, not visible from this point; **25min**), take the first track on the right (still the red/white waymarked **GR 131**, signposted 'LA MESETA'), cutting up

A small reservoir below the Camino Forestal de la Meseta (Picnic 26); Short walk 26 would take you to a similar reservoir — or you could tack it onto the main walk, adding 40 minutes there and back.

into a narrow *barranco*. A gully runs below on your right. Some 100m/yds from the start of the track, go through a chain barrier. After 15 minutes, just after rounding the end of the ridge, climb a path up to the left. Ascending a steep ridge, you'll be brushing through rock-roses. Meeting the track again, you can either cross straight over or take a path 80m/yds further uphill. Surmounting a crest (**1h**), a view unfolds down into another cultivated valley, the **Barranco del Ingenio**.

Turn right for 'LA MESETA' at this junction, climbing on or near the top of the crest all the way up. It's steep. Roque El Cano (photograph page 122) is the enormous rock that disrupts the landscape behind you. A corner of Vallehermoso comes into view, with its *barranco* and, on the far side of the ridge, you look down onto small clusters of homesteads in the Barranco del Ingenio. Nearing **La Meseta**, the path is steeper, narrow in places, sometimes overgrown and skiddy underfoot.

Joining the CAMINO FORESTAL DE LA MESETA (**1h45min**), turn right. *(The Alternative walk joins here, via the path opposite, and the Presa de los Gallos, goal of the Short walk, lies 20 minutes to the left.)* The track skirts the edge of the forest with some pretty wooded spots (Picnic 26). When you

reach the MAIN ROAD, follow it to the left uphill. After about 20 minutes, just before reaching the RESTAURANT CHORROS DE EPINA, turn right on a road signposted 'TAGULUCHE/ALOJERA' (**3h05min**). Ten minutes later, on a hairpin bend, you will climb the small road on the right, up towards a large mast (the **GR 132**). But first make a detour 100m/yds along to the *left*, to enjoy the view: the group of houses you see in the sheltered flat valley below, surrounded by hills, is the hamlet of Tazo. On clear days the twin humps of La Palma appear above the clouds.

Return to the junction and head up the narrow road towards the mast. Three minutes up, turn right downhill on an earthen track (still the red/white waymarked **GR 132**). Three minutes along, take the trail branching off to the right. This GR trail leads all the way to Vallehermoso, with views out across a massive depression of ridges and valleys and over the Embalse de la Encantadora to the right of Vallehermoso.

When you're directly above the town, there is another superb VIEW (**4h20min**) all the way down the Barranco del Valle to the sea. A little over five minutes later, at the first house, you *may* encounter some troublesome unchained dogs. From here a concrete path takes you back down to the centre of **Vallehermoso** (**4h40min**).

124

Walk 27: VALLEHERMOSO • ERMITA SANTA CLARA • PLAYA DE VALLEHERMOSO • VALLEHERMOSO

Distance: 13.5km/8.5mi; 4h30min

Grade: strenuous, with ascents/descents of 750m/2460ft overall. You must be sure-footed and have a head for heights on the descent to Playa de Vallehermoso — it is very steep and gravelly, not recommended for inexperienced walkers. Don't attempt this descent in wet or windy weather. Almost the entire walk follows signposted trails.

Equipment: walking boots, walking stick(s), sunhat, fleece, windproof, long trousers, raingear, picnic, water; swimwear in summer, when the pool is filled — the sea is far too dangerous!

Access: 🚐 to/from Vallehermoso (Timetables 12, 14, 15); journey time from San Sebastián 1h25min. Or 🚗: park in the village by the roundabout.

Shorter walk: Vallehermoso — Ermita Santa Clara — Vallehermoso (9km/5.6mi; 3h20min). Strenuous, with an ascent/descent of about 600m/2000ft. Not recommended in wet weather. Equipment and access as main walk. Follow main walk to the **Santa Clara chapel (1h50min)** and return the same way.

Alternative walk: Vallehermoso — Ermita de Santa Clara — Vallehermoso (13.4km/8.3mi; 4h40min). Access, equipment, grade as Short walk. This circuit avoids the steep and gravelly descent to Playa de Vallehermoso; instead there is a gentle descent through laurel forest. Follow the main walk up to the **Ermita de Santa Clara (1h50min)**. Now turn *left* on the track, away from the *ermita*. If there is no fog, you look down on two small settlements at the end of the world — Tazo and Arguamul. Some 20min along, take a track forking left. This becomes a signposted path running parallel with the track over to the right. Alojera comes into view and the massive cliffs behind it. On the horizon are the crests traversed in Walks 10 and 11. Walk past a *LARGE MAST* (3h05min) for 250m/yds, then pick up Walk 26 in the penultimate paragraph opposite to get back to Vallehermoso (4h40min).

R eaching Vallehermoso is an expedition in itself. Your bus crawls over a mountainous relief carved out with plunging ravines, which leave a skeleton of fine-lined ridges tapering off into the sea. Each unfolding view is better than the last. This exhilarating descent by switchback road is breathtaking! The walk itself gives you commanding panoramas of the normally inaccessible north coast and beyond — on clear days as far as Tenerife and her showpiece, El Teide.

Start out from the *BUS STOP AT THE ROUNDABOUT* in **Vallehermoso**: climb the narrow street at the right of the *BAR CENTRAL (CALLE MAYOR)*. Passing above the *CHURCH*, join the *VALLE GRAN REY ROAD* and follow it left uphill as far as the first bend. Here take the first road on the right, to the *CEMETERY*. Then take the old signposted trail on the right-hand side of the cemetery and descend into the floor of the *barranco*. Cross a

125

white houses in the distance reveals Tamagarda. The path edges its way along the top of the ravine for about 10 minutes, close to the tree line, until you reach a flat crest. If the mist hasn't enveloped you, you'll see the Ermita Santa Clara over to the right.

When you come to an earthen track, turn right and follow it to the **Ermita Santa Clara** (**1h50min**). If the mist lifts, you'll have splendid views from here over the remote village of Arguamul and the group of peaked rocks off its shore, as well as across to La Palma. *(The Shorter walk turns back to Valle-hermoso here and the Alternative walk turns left on the track.)* Continue along the track to the right of the *ermita*, just below the ridge. (Or take the well-defined and protected ridgetop path to the left, which rejoins the track a short way ahead.) Some 30 minutes later, another chapel comes into sight, the **Ermita Nuestra Senora de Coromoto** (**2h20min**), laid bare to the winds on an open crest. Passing it, you descend into a high valley. A rainbow of pastel pinks, browns, greys, mauves and yellows glows out of a bare hillside below. Over on the left, a few stray palms adorning a rocky ridge disclose **Chiguere**, which sits almost unnoticed against the rocks. Ignore the turn-off to this decayed settlement. (But if you want a truly spectacular view of Los Organos from above, *do* take the turn off to this old settlement and, once you reach the houses, cross the hilltop behind them and go on some 100m/yds further to the ridge. The whole structure of Los Organos is visible, from the

footbridge and turn right, to climb towards a couple of houses on the hillside. Roque El Cano (photograph page 122), an enormous spearhead of rock overshadowing the village, commands your attention as you climb.

Keep left at the fork just below the houses. Brushing against the last house, curve round to head up into the **Barranco de la Era Nueva**. The hillsides are freckled with *sabina*, an indigenous juniper. Ignore all paths down to the left. You pass an isolated, abandoned house and then a largish RESERVOIR (**40min**). The trail then crosses an old circular THRESHING FLOOR and begins a series of stream bed crossings, amidst cane, *tabaiba*, brambles, ferns and aromatic *artemisia*. Falcons hover overhead.

After crossing the stream bed for the last time, you enter the evergreen forest and the real ascent begins. Scaling the Teselinde ridge, your view expands to encompass the central spine of the island curling around this immense depression of valleys. A cape of dark cloud, pierced by the occasional ray of sunlight, usually rests on the *cumbre*. Entering heather, the way flattens out. A scattering of

sea to the top. Be careful on this ridge!)

Some 15 minutes later ignore a track to the right to a viewpoint on a hilltop; a minute after that you catch sight of the coast (**2h35min**), and a stunning seascape unfolds. Ridges, serrating the coastline, tumble off into a faintly-green sea. Vallehermoso comes out of hiding, trailing a valley lined with banana groves. The entire countryside is spotted with

sabina. On your right here, you'll spot a sign indicating the start of the zigzagging path down to the beach. (But first, for an even better view of the coast, continue along the track for another 100m/yds, to the **Buenavista** *mirador*.)

Returning to the sign, now begin the descent in the setting shown overleaf. After two minutes, the worst is behind you. *Always* keep your eyes on the path, although the views are irresistible! As well as *sabina*, you'll see a plethora of tubular-stemmed *Ceropegia ceratophora* growing on the slopes. Your view soon stretches all the way up the Barranco del Valle. Closer to the road, the way swings

right, crosses a steep slope and joins a stream bed. As you descend here, watch out for broken glass. After passing below a house (yappy dogs!), take the path to the right, to the road. Turn left downhill for 500m/ yds, to the pool complex at **Playa de Vallehermoso** (**3h35min**; not shown on the map).

Then follow the road gently back uphill to the south. As the after-noon shadows creep across the ravine walls, you amble along-side a valley floor crammed with banana groves and cane. A stream bubbles away below you. Beyond the BOTANICAL GARDEN (which never opened) you come into **Vallehermoso** (**4h30min**).

Coastal scenery near the 'Buenavista' viewpoint

☀ *Appendix*

Information of particular interest to walkers is found on the following pages. We have included as much information about the whole of Tenerife as possible in this book, but do remember that to explore the whole island *on foot*, you will need the companion volume, *Landscapes of Tenerife (Teno • Orotava • Anaga • Cañadas)*.

TOURIST INFORMATION

Both islands have very comprehensive websites, with good maps (including downloadable walking maps) and videos. For **Tenerife** go to www.webtenerife.co.uk; for **Gomera** log on to www.lagomera.travel. The islands' local tourist offices and visitors' centres are another excellent source of (free) information and maps.

BUS, PLANE AND FERRY TIMETABLES

Below is a list of destinations on Tenerife (T) and La Gomera (G) covered by the following timetables. Numbers following places names are *timetable* numbers. There are far more buses *and departures* on Tenerife than those listed here; complete **Tenerife timetables** can be viewed and downloaded from www.titsa.com (the island bus company, with web pages in English). **Gomera timetables** can be checked online at www.guaguagomera. com. Although the website is only in Spanish, just click on 'Horarios' — all the lines are shown, and it is very straightforward to compare times with those in this book to see if there are any changes.

Adeje (T) 5, 9
Agulo (G) 12
Alajeró (G) 13
Arona (T) 4, 6
Arure (G) 11, 16
Boca Tauce (T) 4
Casa de la Seda (G) 11, 16
Caseta de los Noruegos (G) 11
Chipude (G) 11, 14, 16
Cruce de la Zarcita (G) 11
Degollada de Peraza (G) 11, 13

Hermigua (G) 12
Imada turn-off (G) *see* Alajeró
Jerduñe (G) 13, 17
La Calera (G) 11, 16
La Escalona (T) 4, 7
Las Casetas (G) 12
Las Hayas (G) 11, 14, 16
Lomo Blanco (T) 4
Lomo del Balo (G) 11, 16
Los Cristianos (T) 2-4, 7-10, 18; *see also* car ferry timetables, page 133

Los Gigantes (T) 9
Los Granados (G) 11, 16
Pajarito (G) 11
Parador de las Cañadas (T) 4
Playa de las Américas (T) 2-4, 7-10
Playa de San Juan (T) 9
Playa de Santiago (G) 13, 17, 18
Puerto de la Cruz (T) 1, 2
Roque de Agando (G) 11

San Sebastián (G) 11-13; *see also* ferry timetables, page 138
Santa Cruz (T) 1, 3
Santiago del Teide (T) 8
Targa turn-off (G) 13, 16
Valle Gran Rey (G) 11, 16, 18
Vallehermoso (G) 12, 14, 15
Vilaflor (T) 4, 7
Vueltas (G) 11, 16, 18

BUS SERVICES — TENERIFE

1 🚌 102: Santa Cruz to Puerto de la Cruz; *express*; daily

Santa Cruz	La Laguna	Puerto	*Sat/Sun/holidays*
07.40	07.55	08.40	*The times shown at the*
then every 30 minutes at 10 and 40min past the hour until			*left are from Mon to Fri.*
21.00	21.45	22.00	*On Sat/Sun/holidays*
Puerto	**La Laguna**	**Santa Cruz**	*buses are almost as*
06.15	07.00	07.15	*frequent but they depart*
then every 30 minutes at 15 and 45min past the hour until			*at different minutes*
21.15	22.00	22.15	*past the hour.*

2 🚌 343: Costa Adeje to Puerto de la Cruz; *express*; daily

Costa Adeje	Los Cristianos	Puerto	Puerto	Los Cristianos	Costa Adeje
09.00	09.15	11.30	09.00	11.15	11.30
11.30	11.45	14.00	11.25	13.40	13.55
15.30	15.45	18.00	15.25	17.40	17.55
18.00	18.15	20.30	18.00	20.15	20.30

3 🚌 111: Santa Cruz to Costa Adeje; daily

Santa Cruz	La Candelaria	Poris de Abona	Los Cristianos	Costa Adeje
		Mondays to Fridays		
06.55	07.10	07.45	08.20	08.35
		and every 30minutes until		
20.25	20.40	21.15	21.50	22.05
		Saturdays, Sundays and holidays		

Departures from Santa Cruz at 07.05, 09.40, 12.40, 13.15, 15.55, 19.15
Same intermediate and final journey times

Costa Adeje	Los Cristianos	Poris de Abona	La Candelaria	Santa Cruz
		Mondays to Fridays		
06.55	07.10	07.45	08.20	08.35
		and every 30minutes until		
20.25	20.40	21.15	21.50	22.05
		Saturdays, Sundays and holidays		

Departures from Santa Cruz at 08.25, 11.20, 13.55, 14.35, 17.35, 20.45
Same intermediate and final journey times

4 🚌 342: Costa Adeje to Las Cañadas; daily

Costa Adeje station (depart)	09.15	El Portillo (depart)	15.15
Los Cristianos	09.30	Visitors' Centre	15.17
Arona	09.45	Teide cable car	15.40
Vilaflor	10.10	Parador	16.00
Boca Tauce	10.35	Boca Tauce	16.05
Parador	10.45	Vilaflor	16.25
Teide cable car	10.55	Arona	17.00
Visitors' Centre	11.43	Los Cristianos	17.30
El Portillo	11.45	Costa Adeje station	17.45

5 🚌 447: Los Cristianos to Adeje; daily

Los Cristianos	Playa Américas	Adeje	*Sat/Sun/holidays*
06.45	07.00	07.15	*The times shown at the*
and approximately every 30 minutes until			*left are from Mon to Fri.*
21.05	21.20	21.35	*On Sat/Sun/holidays*
Adeje	**Playa Américas**	**Granadilla**	*buses run hourly*
07.00	07.15	07.30	*anywhere from 10min*
and approximately every 30 minutes until			*to 45min past the hour.*
21.15	21.30	22.00	*Check the web for exact times.*

🚌 480: Los Cristianos to Arona; daily*

Los Cristianos	Arona		Arona	Los Cristianos
07.30	07.50		07.00	07.20
09.00	09.20		08.00	08.20
10.00	10.20		09.00	09.20
10.30	10.50		09.30	09.50
and approximately hourly until			and approximately hourly until	
19.30	19.50		20.00	20.20

Check exact departure times on the web: some depart on the hour, others at 5min-30min past the hour; *Sat/Sun/holiday departures less frequent (only every 2-3 hours)*

🚌 482: Los Cristianos to Vilaflor; Sat/Sun/holidays *only*

Los Cristianos	La Escalona	Vilaflor
05.50	06.15	06.25
10.45	11.10	11.20
17.15	17.40	17.50

Vilaflor	La Escalona	Los Cristianos
06.30	06.40	07.05
11.30	11.40	12.05
18.00	18.10	18.35

🚌 460: Costa Adeje to Icod; daily

Costa Adeje	Guía de Isora	Santiago del Teide	Icod de los Vinos
07.45	08.10	08.35	09.10
09.50	10.15	10.40	11.15
11.45	12.10	12.35	13.10
14.10	14.35	15.00	15.35
16.05	16.30	16.55	17.30
18.25	18.50	19.15	19.50
20.00	20.25	20.50	21.25

Icod de los Vinos	Santiago del Teide	Guía de Isora	Costa Adeje
07.45	08.20	08.45	09.10
10.00	10.35	11.00	11.25
11.55	12.30	12.55	13.20
14.05	14.40	15.05	15.30
16.10	16.45	17.10	17.35
18.20	18.55	19.20	19.45
20.10	20.45	21.10	21.35

🚌 473: Los Cristianos to Los Gigantes; daily

Los Cristianos*	Adeje	Playa San Juan	Los Gigantes
06.45	07.15	07.40	08.05
07.15	07.45	08.10	08.35
	and every half hour until		
20.15	20.45	21.10	21.35
	then		
22.15	22.45	23.10	23.35

Los Gigantes	Playa San Juan	Adeje	Los Cristianos**
06.15	06.40	07.05	07.35
06.45	07.10	07.35	08.05
07.30	07.55	08.30	09.00
08.00	08.25	09.00	09.30
	and every half hour until		
21.00	21.25	22.00	22.30
	then		
21.20	21.45	22.20	22.50
21.40	22.05	22.40	23.10
22.30	22.55	23.20	23.45
23.30	23.55	01.20	01.45

Bus passes through Playa de las Américas *10 minutes later; **10 minutes earlier

10 🚐 111: Playa de las Américas — Aeropuerto del Sur; daily

Costa Adeje*	Aeropuerto	Aeropuerto	Costa Adeje**
06.00	06.40	07.00	07.40
	and every 30 minutes		
21.20	22.00	22.00	22.40

Passes through Los Cristianos *15 minutes later; **15 minutes earlier

BUS SERVICES — LA GOMERA

11 🚐 Línea 1: San Sebastián — Valle Gran Rey

San Sebastián	Degollada de Peraza	Cruce de la Zarcita	Pajarito
10.30*	10.50*	10.55*	11.05*
12.00#	12.20#	12.25#	12.35#
15.30#	15.50#	15.55#	16.05#
18.30#	18.50#	18.55#	19.05#
20.30+	20.50+	20.55+	21.05+
21.30=	21.50=	21.55=	22.05=
21.45•	22.05•	22.10•	22.20•

Chipude	Arure	Valle Gran Rey	
11.20*	11.45*	12.20*	
12.50#	13.15#	13.50#	
16.20#	16.45#	17.20#	
19.20#	19.45#	20.20#	
21.20+	21.45+	22.20+	
22.20=	22.45=	23.20=	
22.35•	23.00•	23.35•	

Valle Gran Rey	Arure	Chipude	Pajarito
05.00#	05.35#	06.00#	06.15#
08.00*	08.35*	09.00*	09.15*
13.00#	13.05#	14.00#	14.15#
14.30#	15.05#	15.30#	15.45#
16.30•	17.05•	17.30•	17.45•
18.00#	18.35#	19.00#	19.15#

Cruce de la Zarcita	Degollada de Peraza	San Sebastián	
06.25#	06.30#	06.50#	
09.25*	09.30*	09.50*	
14.25#	14.30#	14.50#	
15.55#	16.00#	16.20#	
17.55•	18.00•	18.20•	
19.25#	19.30#	19.50#	

12 🚐 Línea 2: San Sebastián — Hermigua — Agulo — Vallehermoso

San Sebastián	Hermigua	Agulo	Las Rosas	Vallehermoso
10.30*	11.05*	11.20*	11.35*	11.55*
12.00#	12.35#	12.50#	13.05#	13.25#
15.30#	16.05#	16.55#	17.10#	17.30#
18.30#	19.05#	19.55#	20.10#	20.30#
20.30+	21.05+	21.55+	22.10+	22.30+
21.30=	22.05=	22.55=	23.10=	23.30=
21.45•	22.20•	23.10•	23.25•	23.45•

Vallehermoso	Las Rosas	Agulo	Hermigua	San Sebastián
05.30#	05.50#	06.05#	06.20#	06.55#
07.30+‡	07.50+‡	08.05+‡	08.20+‡	08.55+‡
08.00=•‡	08.20=•‡	08.35=•‡	08.50=•‡	09.25=•‡
13.30#‡	13.50#‡	14.05#‡	14.20#‡	14.55#‡
15.30#‡	15.50#‡	16.05#‡	16.20#‡	16.55#‡
17.00•	17.20•	17.35•	17.50•	18.25•
18.00#	18.20#	18.35#	18.50#	19.25#

* daily (including holidays); = Sat; + Mon-Fri; # Mon-Sat; • Sun; ‡ connection to the airport

3 🚌 Línea 3: San Sebastián — Playa de Santiago — Alajeró

San Sebastián	Peraza Pass	Playa Santiago	Alajeró	
07.00#‡	07.20#‡	07.45#‡	08.05#‡	*Bus continues*
10.30#‡	10.50#‡	11.15#‡	11.35#‡	*to the turn-off*
12.00#‡	12.20#‡	12.45#‡	13.05#‡	*to Imada*
15.30#‡	15.50#‡	16.15#‡	16.35#‡	
17.45#‡	18.05#‡	18.30#‡	18.50#‡	
20.30*‡	20.50*‡	21.15*‡	21.35*‡	
21.30=‡	21.50=‡	22.15=‡	22.35=‡	
21.45•‡	22.05•‡	22.30•‡	22.50√	
Alajeró	**Playa Santiago**	**Peraza Pass**	**San Sebastián**	
05.30#‡	05.45#‡	06.15#‡	06.35#‡	*Bus returns*
07.00*‡	07.15*‡	07.45*‡	08.05*‡	*from the turn-off*
13.30#‡	13.45#‡	14.15#‡	14.35#‡	*to Imada;*
15.30#‡	15.45#‡	16.15#‡	16.35#‡	*arrive early!*
17.30•‡	17.45•‡	18.15•‡	18.35•‡	
19.00#‡	19.15#‡	19.45#‡	20.05#‡	

---

4 🚌 Línea 4: Vallehermoso — Las Hayas — Chipude — La Dama

•eparts **Vallehermoso** 06.30, 12.00 (a) *Mon-Fri only*
•eparts **La Dama** 08.00 (a), 13.30 (a) *Mon-Fri only*
a) connection to San Sebastián at Chipude via Línea 1

---

5 🚌 Línea 5: Vallehermoso — Epina — Alojera

•eparts **Vallehermoso** 05.30, 13.30 *Mon-Fri only*
•eparts **Alojera** 06.30 (a), 14.30 (a) *Mon-Fri only*
a) connection to San Sebastián at Vallehermoso via Línea 2; connection to airport at San
•ebastián via Línea 3 or Línea 7

---

6 🚌 Línea 6: Valle Gran Rey — Airport

•eparts **Valle Gran Rey** *daily, two hours before flights*
•eparts **Airport** *daily, on arrival of flights*

---

7 🚌 Línea 7: San Sebastián — Airport

•eparts **San Sebastián** *daily, 1h45min before flights*
•eparts **Airport** *daily, on arrival of flights*

NTER-ISLAND FLIGHTS

La Gomera can currently be reached by plane from Tenerife Norte or Gran
Canaria; for information/reservations see www.bintercanarias.com.

NTER-ISLAND CAR FERRY SERVICES

Two companies operate car ferries between Los Cristianos on Tenerife and
•an Sebastián on Gomera. Ticket offices open about one hour before sailing
•me. Ferries depart from No 7 on the plan of Los Cristianos on the touring
•nap. Current timetables are shown below; update at the operators' websites.

red Olsen (www.fredolsen.es), Benchijigua Express: sailing time 50min
•eparts Los Cristianos 9.00 *Mon/Tue/Wed/Sat*, 09.30 *Thu/Sun*, 10.00 *Wed*, 12.30 *Thu*, 14.00
Mon/Tue/Sat, 15.00 *Fri/Sun*, 19.00 *Mon/Tue/Fri/Sat/Sun*, 19.30 *Wed*, 20.00 *Thu*
•eparts San Sebastián 07.30 *Mon/Tue/Wed/Sat*, 08.00 *Thu/Sun*, 10.30 *Wed*, 11.00 *Thu*, 12.00
Mon/Tue/Sat, 14.30 *Fri*, 17.30 *Mon/Tue/Fri/Sat/Sun*, 18.00 *Wed*, 18.30 *Thu*

Naviera Armas (naviera-armas.com): sailing time 1h30min
•eparts Los Cristianos 08.45 *daily*, 13.30 *Thu*, 14.00 *Tue/Wed*, 14.30 *Fri*, 17.45 *Mon/Sun*, 18.30
Tue-Fri, 19.00 *Sat*, 21.00 *Sun/Mon*
•eparts San Sebastián 07.00 *daily*, 11.00 *Thu/Fri*, 11.30 *Tue/Wed*, 16.30 *Thu/Fri*, 17.00
Tue/Wed/Sat, 19.30 *Sun/Mon*

Index

Geographical names only are included here; for non-geographical entries, see Contents, page 3. A page number in *italic type* indicates a map; a page number in **bold type** a photograph. Either of these may be in addition to a text reference on the same page. 'TT': Timetables. The approximate pronunciation of village names is shown. (T) Tenerife; (G) La Gomera.

Adeje (T) (Ah-**day**-hay) 17, 18, 50, *52-3,* 54, TT130, 131
Aguamansa (T) (Ah-gwah-**mahn**-sah) 9, 15
Agulo (G) (Ah-**goo**-loh) 11, 32, 118, **119**, *120-1,* 121, TT132
Alajeró (G) (Ah-lah-hay-**roh**) 26, TT132-3
Almáciga (T) (Ahl-**mah**-see-gah) 23
Alojera (G) TT133
Alto de Garajonay *see* Garajonay
Alto del Contadero (G) 29, 30, 86, 87, *112-3*
Anaga Peninsula (T) 20-3
Arafo (T) 13, 18, 19
Araza (T) (Ah-**rah**-thah) 9, 64, **65**, *66-7*
Arico (T) (Ah-**ree**-koh) 19
Arona (T) (Ah-**roh**-nah) 14, **47**, 48, *49,* TT130, 131,
Arure (G) (Ah-**roo**-ray) 10, 24, 34, *70-1,* 72, **73**, 74, 77, 77, TT132
Bajamar (T) (Bah-hah-**mahr**) 20
Barranco (ravine, river bed) (Bah-**rahn**-koh)
  de Agua Jilva (G) 107, *108-9*
  de Argaga (G) *70-1,* 81, 82
  de Arure (G) 10, **69**, *70-1*
  de Benchijigua (G) 11, 92, **94**, *96-7*
  de Contrera (G) *96-7,* 105
  de Guaranet (G) *70-1,* 76
  de Chinguarime (G) *96-7,* 105
  de Erque (G) 10, *70-1,* 85
  de Guarimiar (G) 89, **90**, **92**, **94**, *96-7,* 98
  de Guincho (G) *96-7,* 105
  de Juel 111, *112-3*
  de la Guancha (G) 104, *108-9*
  de la Era Nueva (G) 125, *127*
  de la Matanza *70-1,* 82
  de la Vasa *96-7,* 105
  de las Aguas (T) *60-1,* 62
  de las Casas (G) *108-9, 112-3,* 114; (T) 48, *49*
  de las Lajas (G) 11, 27, **28**, *96-7,* 99, **100**
  de los Castredores (G) *96-7,* 105
  de Masca (G) 9, **13**, 35, *66-7,* **67**, **68**
  de Monteforte (G) 111, *112-3,* 115
  de Ruiz (T) 15
  de Santiago (G) 27, *96-7,* 95, *96-7,* 98
  de Taguluche (G; Valle Gran Rey) *70-1,* 75, 77; (G; Hermigua) 111, *112-3*
  del Agua (G) *70-1,* 80
  del Cedro (G) 37, *112-3,* **115**; (T) *57*
  del Infierno (T) 9, 50-1, **52**, *52-3,* 54, **55**, 66, 69
  del Ingenio (G) 123, *127*
  del Revolcadero (G) 103, *108-9*

del Rincón (G) *108-9*
del Valle (G) 124, *127*
del Valle Gran Rey (G) 69, *70-1,* 80
  Juan de Vera *96-7,* 101, 104
  Madre del Agua (T) *66-7*
  Seco del Natero (T) 64, **65**, *70-1*
Batán (T) (Bah-**tahn**) 21
Benchijigua (G) (Bane-shee-**hee**-gwah) 11, 94, 95, *96-7,* *112-3*
Benijo (T) (Bay-**nee**-hoh) 23
Berruga *96-7,* 101, 102
Boca del Paso (T) *52-3,* 54
Boca Tauce (T) 9, 14, 18, 56, *57,* TT130
Buenavista (T) (Boo-ay-nah-**bees**-tah) 16
Calvario (G) 26, *96-7*
Camino Forestal de Majona (G) 28, 106, **107**, *108-9*
Campamento Madre del Agua (T) *60-1,* 63
Candelaria (T) (Kan-day-**lah**-ree-ah) **20**
Casa de la Seda (G) (**Kah**-sah day lah **Say**-dah) 69, *70-1,* TT132
Casas de Contrera (G) (**Kah**-sahs day Kon-**tray**-rah) *96-7,* 101, 102, **104**, 105
Casas de Cuevas Blancas (G) (day Koo-**ay**-vahs **Blahn**-kahs) 106, **107**, *108-9*
Casas de Jaragán 106, *108-9*
Casas del Joradillo *96-7,* 105
Caseta de los Noruegos (G) 11, 29, 31, 91, 92, *96-7*
Chamorga (T) (Shah-**more**-gah) 22
Chanajiga (T) 9
Chio (T) 9, 18
Chipude (G) (She-**poo**-deh) 25, *70-1,* 81, 82, 84, 85, 86, 88, TT132, 133
Chorros de Epina (G) 11, 34, 123, 124, *127,* TT133
Cruce de la Zarcita (G) 29, 31, 86, 87, *112-3,* TT132
Degollada (pass)
  de Cerrillal *70-1,* 83
  de Guajara (T) 59, *60-1*
  de Peraza *see under* Mirador
  del Tanque (G) *96-7,* 99, **100**
El Apartadero (G) (Ayl Ah-pahr-tah-**day**-roh) *70-1,* 85
El Aserradero (T) *52-3,* 54
El Azadoe (G) 94, 95, *96-7,* 98
El Cabezo (G) 94, 95, *96-7,* 98
El Cabrito (G) 103, **104**, *108-9*
El Cedro (G) (Ayl **Say**-droh) 11, 29, 86, 87, **88**, *112-3,* 115, **117**

134

El Cercado (G) (Ayl Thair-**kah**-doh) 25, *70-1*, 84-5
El Guro (G) (Ayl **Gu**-roh) 69, *70-1*, 83
El Lagar (T) 9
El Palmar (G) (Ayl Pahl-**mahr**) 110, *112-3;* (T) 17
El Portillo (T) 14, 18, TT130
El Rumbazo (G) (Ayl Room-**bah**-thoh) 26, 89, 91, 93, *96-7*
El Sombrero (G) **26-7**, *96-7*
El Teide (T) **1**, **15**, **19**, TT130
El Tión (G) (Ayl Tee-**ohn**) *112-3*, 118, *120-1*, **121**
Embalse (reservoir) (Aym-**bahl**-say)
de Agulo 118, *120-1*
de Amalahuigue (G) 32, *112-3*, 118, *120-1*
de Chejelipes (G) **28**, *112-3*
de Izcagüe (G) **28**, *112-3*
de la Encantadora (G) 123-4, *127*
de Mulagua (G) *112-3*, 116
Enchereda (G) (En-shay-**ray**-dah) 110, *112-3*, **114**
Epina (G) (Ay-**pee**-nah) 34, *127*, TT133
Ermita (chapel) (Ehr-**mee**-tah)
de las Nieves (G) 11, 27, *96-7*, 100
de los Reyes (G) *70-1*, 83
de San Juan (G; Benchijigua) **94**, *96-7*, 98, *112-3;* (G; Hermigua) *112-3*, 117
del Santo (G) *see under* Mirador
Nuestra Señora de Coromoto (G) 126, *127*
Nuestra Señora de Guadalupe (G) *70-1*, 81, **82**, 83
Nuestra Señora de Lourdes (G) 86, 87, **87**, *112-3*
San Salvador (G) 10, *70-1*, 74, **75**, 76
Santa Clara (G) 125, 126, *127*
Fasnia (T) (**Fahs**-nya) 19
Garachico (T) (Gah-rah-**she**-koh) 16
Garajonay (and National Park) (G) **10**, 29, 30, 32, 77, 86, 87, 91, *96-7*, *112-3*
Gerián (G) (Jeh-ree-**ahn**) *70-1*, 81, **82**
Granadilla (T) (Grah-nah-**deel**-yah) 19
Guarimiar (G) (Goo-ahr-ee-mee-**ahr**) 91, **92**, 93, 95, *96-7*
Guergues, Finca de (T) 64, **65**, *70-1*
Guía de Isora (T) (**Gee**-ah day Ee-**so**-rah) 18
Güimar (T) (Gwee-**mahr**) 19
Hermigua (G) (Air-**mee**-gah) 31, 110, 111, *112-3*, 115, **116**, 117, *120-1*, TT132
Icod de los Vinos (T) (**Ee**-kod day lohs **Bee**-nohs) **16**
Ifonche (T) (Ee-**fohn**-shay) 9, *52-3*, 54, **55**
Igueste (T) (Ee-**gwes**-tay) 23
Imada (G) (Ee-**mah**-dah) 91, 93-4, *96-7*, 98
Jardín de las Creces (G) 11, *70-1*, 77, 79, 123
Jerduñe (G) (Hair-**doon**-yay) *96-7*, 101
Juego de Bolas 32, 35, *96-7*, *112-3*, 118, *120-1*
La Cabezada (T) 64, **65**, *66-7*
La Caldera (T) 9, 15
La Calera (G) (Lah Kah-**lay**-rah) *70-1*, 72, 83, TT132-3

La Crucita (T) 18, **19**
La Escalona (T) (Lah Es-kah-**loh**-nah) 9, *52-3*, 55, TT131
La Fortaleza (G) 10, **31**, *70-1*, 84, 85
La Gerode (G) 107, *108-9*
La Laguna (T) (Lah Lah-**goo**-nah) 21, TT130
La Laja (G) (Lah **Lah**-hah) *96-7*, 99, **100**
La Mérica (G) *70-1*, 72-3
La Meseta (and Camino Forestal) (G) 11, 34, 123, **124**, *127*
La Orotava (T) (Lah Oh-roh-**tah**-vah) 15
La Palmita, La (G) (Lah Pahl-**mee**-tah) 11, 32, *112-3*, 118, 119, *120-1*
La Tabaiba (T) 17
La Vizcaína (G) (Lah Bees-kay-**ee**-nah) *70-1*, 84
Laguna Grande (G) 11, 29, 30, 34, *70-1*
Las Arenas Negras (T) 9
Las Bodegas (T) (Lahs Boh-**day**-gahs) 22-3
Las Cañadas (National Park, Visitors' Centre, Parador) (T) 9, 14, 18, 38, 52, **57**, 58, 59, *60-1*, TT130
Las Canteras (T) (Lahs Kahn-**tay**-rahs) 20, 22
Las Carboneras (T) (lahs Kahr-boh-**nay**-rahs) 21
Las Casetas (G) 110, *112-3*, **114**
Las Hayas (G) (Lahs **Aie**-ahs) 10, 25, 29, 30, *70-1*, 77, 80, 123, TT133
Las Lajas (T) 9, 14
Las Mimbreras (G) 86, *112-3*
Las Rosas, Las (G) (Lahs **Roh**-sahs) 32, *112-3*, 118, *120-1*, TT132
Llano de Las Mesas (T) 44, **45**
Lo del Gato (G) (**Lo** dayl **Gah**-toh) 95, *96-7*
Lomo Blanco (T) 14, 59, *60-1*, 63, TT130
Lomo del Balo (G) (**Loh**-moh dayl **Bah**-loh) *70-1*, **79**, 84, TT132
Los Aceviños (G) (Lohs Ah-say-**been**-yohs) **2**, 86, *112-3*
Los Azulejos (T) 14
Los Cristianos (T) (Lohs Krees-t'**yan**-ohs) 14, **17**, 37, 38, 44, **45**, **46**, TT130, 131, 133
town plan touring map
Los Descansaderos (G) (Lohs Dehs-kan-sah-**day**-rohs) *70-1*, 80, 84
Los Gigantes (T) (Lohs Hee-**gahn**-tays) 17, 66, TT131
Los Granados (G) (Lohs Grah-**nah**-dohs) *70-1*, 77, 80, TT132
Los Manantiales (G) (Lohs Mahn-ahn-tee-**ahl**-ays) *70-1*, **88**
Los Pajares (T) 64, **65**, **65**
Los Roques (T) 29, 31, **32-3**, 99, **107**
Los Silos (T) (Lohs **See**-lohs) 16
Masca (T) (**Mahs**-kah) 9, **12-3**, 17, *66-7*, 68
Mériga (G) 11, 30
Mirador (viewpoint) (Mee-rah-**door**)
A Lazcano (G) 110, *112-3*, 114, TT132
Acequía Larga (T) 51, *52-3*
Barranquillos Asomada (G) 34

Buenavista (G) 126, *127*, **128**
Cruz del Carmen (T) 21, 22
de Abrante (G) 32, 118, 119, *120-1*
de Agulo (G) 118, **119**, *120-1*
de Alojera (G) 34
de Cumbres (T) 19
de Igualero (G) 25
de Ortuño (T) 19
de San Pedro (T) 15
de Tajaque (G) 29
de las Chamucadas (T) 22
Degollada de Peraza (G) 11, **26-7**, *96-7*,
　99, 100, *112-3*, TT132
del Drago (G) 25
El Bailadero (G) 29, 31; (T) 22, **23**,
El Palmarejo (G) 24
El Rejo (G) 29, 31
Ermita del Santo (G) 10, 24-5, 34, *70-1*, 72,
　73, 74, 75
Minas de San José (T) 14
Narices del Teide (T) 18
Pico de las Flores (T) 9, 19
Pico del Inglés (T) 21, 22
Piedra la Rosa (G) **9**, 15
Pino Gordo (T) 14
Rose de las Piedras (G) 33
Tabonal (T) 14
Montaña (mountain)
de Guajara (T) **58**, 59, *60-1*
del Cedro (T) 56, *57*
Guaza (T) 44, *45*, **46**
Monte Los Frailes (T) 9, 19
Monteforte (G) *see* Hermigua
Paisaje Lunar (T) 59, *60-1*, **62-3**
Pajarito (G) 29, 31, 91, *96-7*, *112-3*, TT132-3
Pastrana (G) (Pahs-**trah**-nah) 11, 26, 94,
　95, *96-7*
Pavón (G) (Pah-**bohn**) 10, *70-1*, 85
Pico Viejo (T) 18, *56-7*, **58**
Piedras Amarillas (T) 9, 14, 59, *60-1*
Playa (beach) (**Ply**-yah)
de Argarga (G) *70-1*, 81
de la Caleta (G) 11, 110, *112-3*
de la Guancha (G) 103, 104, *108-9*
de Vallehermoso (G) 33, 125, **126**, *127*,
　128
del Cabrito (G) **104**
del Medio (G) *96-7*, 105
Playa de las Américas (T) (**Ply**-yah day lahs
　Ah-**may**-ree-kahs) 14, 18, 37, 38, TT130-2
town plan *touring map*
Playa de Masca *66-7*, 68
Playa de Santiago (G) (**Ply**-yah day Sahn-
　tee-**ah**-goh) 26, 37, 89, 90, *96-7*, 101,
　103, 105, TT132-3
Presa de los Gallos 11, 123, *127*
Puerto de la Cruz (T) (Poo-**air**-toh day lah
　Krooth) 15, TT130
Puerto de Santiago (G) (Poo-**air**-toh day
　Sahn-tee-**ah**-goh) 17
Punta (point) (**Poon**-tah)
de Pejereyes (G) *70-1*, **77**

de Teno (T) 16
del Fraile (T) 16
Punta del Hidalgo (T) (**Poon**-tah dayl Ee-
　dahl-goh) 20
Raso de la Bruma (G) 11, 30, 34, *70-1*
River, River bed *see* Barranco
Rock *see* Roque
Roque (rock) (**Roh**-kay)
de Agando (G) **10**, 11, 29, **94**, *96-7*, 99,
　100
de las Animas (T) 21
de la Zarcita (G) **1**
de Ojila (G) **32-3**, *96-7*, **100**
de San Pedro (G) 31, *112-3*, 116
de Taborno (T) **21**
del Conde (T) **47**, **48**, *49*
El Cano (G) 33, *120-1*, **122**, *127*
Roque de las Bodegas (T) 23
Roque Negro (T) 22
Roques (rocks) (**roh**-kays)
de García (T) 14, **15**, *60-1*
del Cedro (T) 56, *57*, **58**
Rosa de las Piedras (G) (**Roh**-sah day lahs
　Pee-**ay**-drahs) 11, 33, *120-1*
San Andrés (T) (**Sahn Ahn**-drays) 23
San Juan (G) (San Hu-**an**) 17, TT131
San Juan de la Rambla (T) (San Hu-**an** day
　lah **Rahm**-blah) 15
San Sebastián (G) (**Sahn** Say-bahs-t'**yan**)
　7, 28, 103, 106, *108-9*, TT132-3
town plan *touring map*
Santa Cruz (T) (**Sahn**-tah **crooth**) 23,
　TT130
Santiago del Teide (T) (Sahn-tee-**ah**-goh
　dayl Tay-**ee**-day) 17, *62-3*, TT131
Seima (G) (Say-**ee**-mah) *96-7*, 101, 105,
　108-9
Taborno (T) (Tah-**bohr**-noh) 21
Tacalcuse (G) *96-7*, 101, **102**
Taco (G) (**Tah**-koh) 26
Tacoronte (T) (Tah-koh-**rohn**-tay) 20
Taganana (T) (Tah-gah-**nah**-nah) **23**
Taguluche (Tah-goo-**loo**-chay) (G;
　Hermigua) 34, 110, *112-3*; (G; Valle Gran
　Rey) 10, 25, *70-1*, 74, **75**, 77
Tamagarda (G) (Tah-mah-**gahr**-dah) 33
Tamaimo (T) (Tah-**my**-moh) 17
Targa (G) (**Tahr**-gah) 10, **89**, 90, *96-7*,
　TT132-3
Tegueste (T) (Tay-**gways**-tay) 20
Tejina (T) (Tay-**hee**-nah) 20
Teno Alto (T) (**Tay**-noh **Ahl**-toh) 17
Valle Gran Rey (G) (**Bahl**-yay Grahn **Ray**)
　24, 29, 37, *70-1*, 72, **80**, 81, 83, TT132-3
Vallehermoso (G) (Bahl-yay-hair-**moh**-soh)
　33, 118, *120-1*, **122**, 123, 124, 125, **126**,
　127, **128**, TT132-3
Valley *see* Barranco
Viewpoint *see* Mirador
Vilaflor (T) (Bee-lah-**floor**) 14, 59, *60-1*, 63,
　TT130, 131
Vueltas (G) *70-1*, 72, TT133